You Are
ALREADY
DEAD

JERRY LEE JOHNSON

ISBN 978-1-0980-4430-5 (paperback)
ISBN 978-1-0980-4431-2 (digital)

Christian Faith Publishing, Inc.
832 Park Avenue
Meadville, PA 16335
www.christianfaithpublishing.com

Printed in the United States of America

Contents

Introduction

Why did I use the title for this book, *You Are Already Dead*? I used this title to illustrate my point as to what I and multitudes of other people believe is the spiritual state of all humanity. You are already dead! You may be asking, what the heck does that mean? I am not dead. Do you see me breathing? Do you hear me talking? Do you see me flipping you the finger? I am writing this book because men, women, and children all over the world are dying every day without any understanding or any kind of hope. Without any kind of assurance of what will happen to them when they die. This is probably the most profound of mysteries we will face in this life. So many people are living their lives in the fear of death. Some are so fearful, they are crippled by it. In this book, I hope to address what really happens to us when we do actually die.

I, like countless other men and women, believe that there is a heaven. A wonderful, awesome, beautiful, peaceful, and eternal place. I do also believe there is a hell. A place of eternal fire, torment, torture, and utter horror. I believe there is a God, the creator of the heavens and the earth and the creator of man. I also believe there is a devil. The deceiver and corrupter of the whole world, the mortal enemy of all mankind. I believe there is an unseen battle going on between heaven and hell for our eternal souls. I believe when we die, we will all end up in either that heaven or in that hell for eternity. In this book, I want to address why I, and so many others, believe these things to be the truth.

I want to address the most serious question anyone could ever ask. If you're honest, you and virtually every person who has ever lived has thought about it. Every one of us has asked this question at some point in their lives. What will happen to me when I die? Will I go to heaven? Will I go to hell? Will I just return to the cosmos? Will I be reincarnated and get another chance? Or will I just cease to be? What really happens to us when we die? I believe you can know the answer to that question. I also believe you actually have the choice of where you will spend your eternity when you do leave this world behind. I believe there are answers to all these questions. You can have a clear understanding. You do not have to fear death! You do not have to fear spending all eternity in that horrible, horrible place called hell! You can also have the assurance that you will spend your eternity in that wonderful place called heaven. What kind of peace would that knowledge give to the scores of people who live in that paralyzing fear? How much peace, how much hope, would that kind of understanding give to you?

We Will All Die!

Death is a really serious topic to tackle in a book, and "We Will All Die" is a very direct title to start it with. This is, though, a subject that will eventually affect every person on this planet. This one subject can affect people in many different and adverse ways. We will all die! This is an undisputable fact! Whether it be today, tomorrow, or thirty years from now, we will all face death. That fabled grim reaper will come knocking on our door. No one can live forever; we will all succumb to its eternal grasp. Death is not a respecter of age, gender, color, nationality, or religion. White, black, rich, poor, Christian, atheist, Hindu, Islamic, Buddhist—it does not matter! We will all one day take our last breath. This mortal body will die and decay.

It would probably be somewhat easier to face if we knew we were going to live out our lives to a ripe old age. Then when we are old, weak, and not really productive anymore, face death and that monumental question. What really happens to me when I die? Unfortunately, in this very unpredictable world of circumstance, we are not guaranteed to be breathing five minutes from now. We are all here for a little while and then gone. This life is very short, and for some, even shorter. That accident you passed yesterday in which a man was killed, he had no clue when he got dressed for work that morning that it was going to be his last. The carload of teenagers who ran their car under a semi-trailer and were killed, they were just out partying and having fun. The plane that crashed into the ocean, all those people just gone. They had no idea that was going to be their fate. The young man who was killed in a motorcycle accident. The mother and her young baby run over by a little old lady. That forty-seven-year-old friend who dropped dead on the bathroom floor from a massive heart attack. The family member or friend who found out they had cancer and were gone after a few short weeks or months. Even my twenty-five-year-old son, who just went swimming one day with a friend, got caught in a riptide, and drowned. All these examples are based on real people and real instances. Just a few that I personally know about. I'm sure you have had similar experiences you know about personally as well.

Not one of these people, when they got up that final morning, realized it was going to be their last. Death comes to us all! With that said, how will you answer that most important, eternal question? What will happen to you when you take your final breath? There is a lot of speculation out there. Well, I hope I am going to heaven, if it exists. I'm going to a better place, whatever place they think that to be. Another, I'm going to just cease to exist when I die, I'm just going to be gone. Someone else may say, I am going to become part of the cosmos and float off into space. Or I will be reborn and do it all over again until I get it right. Some believe they will be reincarnated and become some sort of animal. So don't eat a steak, or you may be eating Uncle Carl. You may even run into the occasional moron who says, I'm going to go to hell, take over, and we're going to have a party. Others may be basing their eternity on some vision someone said they had in a cave. Or a visitation of what they may have believed to be an angel talking to them. The problem with these types of belief systems is, first of all, they are usually based on the word of one person and what they believe to be true. They are based on human speculation or human theory. With no concrete evidence to prove they are the real thing or, in reality, are false. I don't know about you, but this is one area where we absolutely cannot afford to be wrong.

We are talking about forever, our eternity. I don't want to base my entire eternity on someone else's speculation or man-made theories. I say it this way because there is a way for you to know for certain what will happen to you when you die. This statement is not based on the theory of just one man, on speculation, or based on the vision of one man. What I am talking about is based on absolute truth and reality. It is based on the experiences of thousands of people over thousands of years. It's based on the documented history of people and their personal and corporate experiences. It is based on over 2,000 prophecies, foretold over thousands of years. Prophecies that were fulfilled to the smallest detail. Which in itself is virtually impossible. Thousands of absolutely impossible things done in men and women's lives. Miracles done that defy human understanding and logic. All documented and given to us as proof that these things which have been revealed to us are absolutely real.

God also places in us, his children, a personal assurance that what we believe in is the truth. Not only this, I also base my assurance on my own personal experiences, the remarkable things I have experienced in my own life over the years. Things God has revealed to me personally, things I have seen and heard myself. Awesome things I have seen God do in mine and others' lives. These personal experiences have also given me even more assurance. More faith that what I am trusting in for my eternity is real. I have friends who have said to me, "You believe what you believe because you have faith in them." They said this in defense of what they believed to be true themselves. Their response was, "I believe what I believe to be true because I have faith in them too." The problem with this type of thinking is, just because you believe in something or have faith something, does not make it a reality.

There are people who believe in or have faith that vampires, werewolves, and aliens exist too, but that does not make them a reality. That type of faith would be considered a blind faith. There is nothing, no real evidence to prove they are real. I have faith in the things I believe because they have been proven to be absolute truth to multitudes of people in so many different ways. What proof do you have that what you are believing in for your eternity is true? Just because you may believe when you die you are just gone. You are just going to be in blackness or just cease to be, does not mean it's going to happen. Believe me when I say there have been and there are much smarter and wiser men than me who have believed, testified to, and still believe the things I am saying to you are the truth.

My mother passed away from cancer this past year. She put up a strong fight with three bouts with it, but it finally took her. She was definitely a very unique woman. She even put diapers on her weird little dog because she could not potty-train him. I guess that was easier than cleaning up doggy doo. She had her many quirks, as most of us do. She was stuck in her ways, some right, some wrong, as most of us are. She was far from perfect, as all of us are. But because of the hope she had, the hope most of her children and grandchildren have, for a heavenly eternity, there were actually very few tears shed at her funeral. Not because we were not extremely sorrowed by the loss of our mother. But because we are assured that she is in heaven, and we will eventually be together again for all eternity. Most of the tears shed were from the people who did not have the eternal hope I have been talking about. We will all die. You are going to die. I am going to die, and it could be today. Are you ready to meet that grim reaper if he comes calling? Are you truly ready to meet your maker? Do you have a sure hope for your eternity?

I do, I have that hope. The difference in my own life is, if I die today, I am ready. I know without any doubt, if I were to die today, I will be in God's holy heaven forever. Because of that, I don't fear it. I have an eternal, heavenly hope. The hope I have for my eternal future is exciting. I am actually looking forward to it. I would be lying if I said I wasn't little apprehensive about the dying process. But I do have a longing to be in my heavenly home. You may be thinking that's a little crazy. How can someone even talk that way about dying? How can I talk like this? Because of the promises God has given to us in his Word. Because I have been assured in God's Word, I will be reunited with my son again. I am going to be with my mother again. I will see my stepfather again. I will get to see my grandparents and my great grandparents again. I am going to be with all those who have gone before me. Those who have passed, those who also had this same hope for their eternity. My destiny has been laid out for me. I know where and with whom I will spend the rest of eternity. Because of this, I have genuine peace about leaving this body and this world behind. I have security, I don't have to worry about it, and I don't have to fear it. Wouldn't that be a much better way to your live?

Spirit, Soul, Body

Who am I and what am I really composed of? Is there really something more to us than just this physical body? Do we have a spirit or a soul? Or are we just this fleshly being that is here for a little while and then just gone? In this chapter, I will attempt to address these questions. I truly hope, after answering them, it will clarify these commonly misunderstood topics. We are a very complex being. More complex than any other living thing in this world. Only God himself knows it all, but he, through his Word (the Bible), has given us some insight into these things. What I have found through God's Word, and my research, is most theologians and most religions agree that man is made up of a lot more than just a physical body. Most believe we are made up of three distinct components. The three components that make us what and who we are: our body, our mind, and our spirit or soul. For instance, the Bible, referring to the three parts of our being, says in the book of 1 Thessalonians 5:23, "May God himself, the God of peace sanctify you through and through. May your whole *spirit, soul* and *body* be kept blameless at the coming of our Lord Jesus Christ."

Our body, of course, is the flesh and blood part of us. Which is comprised of our physical body, our brain, organs, cells, etc. On this part, everyone must agree is going to die and decay. The human body eventually wears out or suffers trauma, to the point it can no longer sustain itself. The soul: most agree that our soul is what gives us our personality. Our soul is likely made up of three major components, our mind, our will, and our emotions. Our minds have a conscious part and a subconscious part. The conscious part is where our thinking and reasoning skills are said to come from. Our subconscious is where our feelings and emotions come from.

The spirit is said to be the part of our makeup that gives us purpose and meaning. It allows us to love one another from the deepest parts of our being. There are those out there who may argue that the spirit and soul are two distinct, separate entities. There are also many who believe they are one and the same. Whether two parts or one, most religions believe and teach, however, that the soul or spirit of a man does not die. This spirit lives on after our flesh and blood body dies. I believe, like countless others have for thousands of years, that our spirit does live on. Our spirit or soul leaves this mortal body when it can no longer sustain itself. Your spirit will live on somewhere forever!

I have had the profound experience of actually looking directly into the eyes of two people at the exact instant they died. That is a very strange feeling, I have to admit. I'm sure there are those who have had this experience many more times than me. Those like my sister-in-law, being a hospice nurse. I'm sure she has seen this more times than she would like to admit. What made the most impact on me though was actually seeing the light in their eyes fade away and go dark. It was like someone reached inside them and turned off a light switch. I believe this was a visible evidence of their spirit leaving their body. The source of energy that powered their bodies suddenly turned off. I have heard of studies that have been done which monitored the exact moment of a person's death. The people who were being studied lost a measurable amount of weight the instant they died. Something triggered a weight loss that could not be explained with any sound scientific explanation.

There have also been many out-of-body experiences which have been documented over the years. Remarkable and unexplainable experiences described by people who have died and were brought back to life. Seeing themselves floating out of their own bodies. Later, after being revived, describing inexplicable things. Things there is no possible way they could have known in the physical condition they were in. They were dead! There have been books written and movies made about several of these people who have had these experiences, both children and adults.

Some of these recalled their spirit being taken to a beautiful, peaceful, wonderful place they described as heaven. Some say they were taken by angels into the presence of Jesus. Some recalled seeing family members, those who had died years before. Even family members who had died before they were born but were still somehow able to recognize them. Others described what the doctors and nurses were doing and saying as they floated above them. All while they were working feverishly trying to save their life. They have reported in their experiences what family members were doing and saying in other rooms.

They described things that are impossible for them to know. Some also described horrible experiences of demons, darkness, terror, torment, and being dragged to hell. My stepfather had not one, but two similar out-of-body experiences. He had heart problems and died not once, but twice, several years apart. Both times, he was miraculously revived. He described to me in some detail the experiences he had when he died. The first was a blissful, peaceful experience in which he described to me walking down a perfectly smooth dirt path in a beautiful, heavenly place. Everything he could see was filled with beautiful flowers, in colors more vibrant than anything he had ever seen here. Green grass as smooth as velvet and a peace he could not describe. All while holding on to someone's or something's hand, walking over a hill, toward a bright light. For him to describe anything this way was strange. He was a big, burly, no-nonsense ex-marine. The second time he died, he had a dramatically different out-of-body experience. He described his experience to be the exact opposite of his first one. The second he described as being full of darkness, terror, and utter horror, which shook him to his core. His first experience was so beautiful and peaceful, he didn't want to come back. His second experience was so horrible, he was screaming for someone to save him.

I believe there are biblical reasons his experiences were so different the first and second time. This delves into some deeper spiritual things that I will try and clarify a little more in the chapters to come. With as many documented cases as there are of these out-of-body experiences, and so many similarities to these experiences, in my opinion, there must be some validity to them. After all, these people are the ones who have been the closest to seeing what is on the other side. They are the ones who died and came back. There will always be someone out there who will try to explain these experiences away or put a scientific spin on them. Doctors and psychologists will sometimes use some psychological explanation or scientific term for these experiences. But maybe we should just take them for what they are. These people crossed over from life to death. From the physical world into the spiritual world, then stepped back into life again. Maybe we should try to glean from their experiences and learn a little more about the other side. I believe these many documented experiences are yet another proof that there is a whole lot more to this life than what we can see with our physical eyes.

We are more than just a physical being that lives in this world for a little while and is just gone. We all have a spirit, the part of you that makes you who you are. That part of us that energizes and keeps this mortal body alive. The part of us that lives on somewhere when it leaves this body. *You* will leave this mortal body, and *you* will continue to live in the spirit somewhere forever. This leaves us again with that monumental question: What really happens to me when I die? Where will my spirit go? Where will I spend eternity? I believe most of us just go about our everyday lives and try not to even think about it. Death can be a very scary subject. But what if we wait too long to address this question in our own lives? How can we know if we will experience the blissful, peaceful, and wonderful sensation that some experienced? Or whether we will experience the darkness, terror, and utter horror that others described?

Once we cross over from life to death, it's done, it's too late. There is no way we can change our destiny. Not very many of us get a do over, a second chance to make things right, like my stepfather. It's while we are still here, living in this mortal body, we have our only opportunity to change our eternal destiny. Wouldn't that be an awesome thing to know? Wouldn't it be an awesome feeling not to have to fear it? To have an assurance, a sure hope for your eternity? I have some really good news for you. You can know what will happen to you when you die. You can know without any doubt where you will spend your eternity. The choice is actually yours; it's all in your hands. The ball is in your court.

There Is a Devil

There was a quote from a very popular movie that aired several years ago, and one of the lines really stuck with me. The actor, playing the role of a very evil guy, said, "The greatest deception ever conceived, is the devil has made people believe, that he does not exist." This was a line from a movie, but unfortunately in the reality we live in, it is a very real and scary truth. People, I believe for the most part, don't take the reality of a devil very seriously at all. Why? Because he has done a really good job of actually deceiving people, as the quote states. He has, in reality, made people believe that he does not exist. Countless movies that have depicted him as some mythological creature who lives only in the movies. A fictional character who has no real impact on our daily lives. This is, in my opinion, a deception straight from hell. We have been desensitized to the fact that there is a very real, powerful, and very, very evil creature out there, wreaking havoc on our world. In the Bible, the devil or Satan is referred to well over a hundred and fifty times. He is referred to as our enemy, Lucifer, the devil, Satan, the great deceiver, and the father of lies, among other things. His sole objective is to destroy us, kill us, and drag all mankind to hell along with him. The devil is not just mentioned in Christian circles. He is also referred to in Islam as the shaitan or Iblis and in Buddhism as Mara, just to name a couple. The devil is all mankind's mortal enemy.

In 1 Peter 5:8, the Bible says, "Be alert and of sober mind, for your enemy the devil prowls around like a roaring lion, seeking someone to devour."

The scary thing is, the evil depictions of the devil, in some of these horror movies you may have watched over the years, does not even scratch the surface of how horrible and evil he really is. Think back to some of those really scary, horror movies. The ones that scared you so badly, you couldn't sleep for a day or two. You can probably still see some of those horrible scenes years later. Those detestable images that somehow got seared into your mind. Now consider the horror that was depicted in these movies is just a tiny glimpse of something that is very real. He is at work all around us constantly, and his primary goal is to ultimately destroy you! We may not be able to see the devil or his horde of demons with our human eyes. But you don't have to look very hard to see evil working very actively in our world.

People, in what are referred to as the Bible times, were very quick to recognize that many of the afflictions they suffered were direct attacks from the devil and his horde of demons. There are many references in the Bible of people having sicknesses or diseases that were said to be caused by demon possession. The same things the medical community of our day has medical and psychological terms and names for were then described as being caused by demons or the devil. So where did this devil and the demons come from? Who is he really? And why does he want to destroy mankind and cause us so much pain, misery, and fear?

According to the Bible, Satan or Lucifer actually at one time was an angel of God. He was one of the highest-ranking angels in the heavenly realms. He was an archangel in charge of music and all the praise and worship in heaven. He was so powerful, beautiful, and so high-ranking, he became prideful. Prideful to the point he started comparing himself to God. He even set himself up as God. He, and his angel followers, had been leaving their rightful place in heaven. The Bible says they started visiting earth, dominating the people. They were having sex with the women and having children with them. Forcing people to worship them as gods and, according to the Bible, doing things that ought not to be done. The devil and his fallen angel followers rebelled against God. The devil eventually started a war against God and his angels. He was defeated by God. The devil and his demon horde were cast out of heaven and cursed.

In Genesis 6:4, the Bible says the Nephilim were on the earth in those days and also afterward when the sons of God (the fallen angels) went to the daughters of humans and had children by them. They were the heroes of old, men of renown.

These were the giants referred to of that time. If you have any church background at all, you have probably heard the story of David and Goliath from the Bible. Goliath was the giant that King David killed with the slingshot. He was said to be a descendant of this race of giants. The Bible calculations estimated him to be around nine feet tall. He was said to have had six fingers on each hand and six toes on each foot.

We hear today, in movies and books, about mythological beings. So-called gods and powerful beings that were supposedly present in ancient times. Stories from the past that somehow made it all the way to present times. Many of these stories, pictures, and books handed down from generations past came from many different parts of the world. All describing mythological beings, deities, or gods that lived thousands of years ago with surprising consistency. Describing these powerful beings that interjected themselves into the lives of human beings, these deities were feared and worshiped as gods. They forced themselves on people, they made the people worship them. They erected statues, altars, and built temples in their honor. These deities were said to have had power and authority in varying degrees over the world, the elements, and had power over human beings. They were said to have had sexual relations with the women of earth, and children were born to them. These children grew to be the giants of that time. Some were said to have had extraordinary strength. Some were given powers and wisdom not common to mortal man. There have been quite a few movies and television shows made even in the last few years about these mythical gods of the past. Most depicting the exploits of these powerful beings and the special powers, strength, and wisdom given to the children they had with an earthly mother.

Some of the most prominent or most well-known of these deities or immortal beings was Zeus. Zeus was said to be the most powerful of the gods. He was said to be the god of the sky and Olympus, which was the heavenly home of all the gods. He had power over the weather and threw thunderbolts when he was not happy! Second was Poseidon, god of the sea. He was the second most powerful after Zeus. He was said to live in a palace under the sea. He caused earthquakes when he was unhappy! Apollo was said to be the god of healing and music. He was an archer and hunted with a bow made of silver. Aphrodite was the goddess of love and beauty and was the protector over the sailors. Hera was the goddess of love, marriage, heaven, the air, and motherhood of women. Athena was a Greek goddess of wisdom, tactics, and handicrafts. These are just a few of those immortal gods that were said to live thousands of years ago. I'm sure we have all heard these names, read books about them, or seen movies which describe them and some of their activities as passed down in mythology. I just wanted to give a few examples of these mythological deities. Though these deities are not relevant or present in our society today, some cultures still worship some of them. Many false religions started with the worship of these deities.

Now think about the many similarities between the fallen angels the Bible talks about and the stories of the mythological gods of the past. The Bible describes the fallen angels as doing exactly the same things the mythological gods were said to have done. Now consider the possibility that they were one and the same. Call me crazy, but I believe some of the stories about these ancient gods did actually have some validity to them. I believe some of them started with some kind of reality or truth. I believe the devil and the demons were those mythological deities. This is of course speculation on my part, but in my opinion, it's more like putting well-fitting pieces of a puzzle together. I say this because if these stories did actually have some truth to them, it gives more validity to the Bible's description of where the devil came from. Over time, things of course do get skewed and exaggerated. But I don't believe they were all just made up in someone's over-imaginative mind. So where did all these stories come from? Where did these beings come from? Why did they have so much power? Why were some of them much more powerful than the others? And why are they not still active in society today? I believe that every one of these questions was answered for us a long time ago in the Bible. It describes exactly where these beings came from. Why they had these powers over man and the elements. Why some were more powerful than others, and why they are not still active in our world today.

I mentioned before that Satan had a very prominent position in heaven, a very high rank. Just as it is in the military, I believe all these heavenly beings, the angels, have a ranking system. With that rank just like in the military, a higher rank means more power and authority. A general of course has much more power and authority than, say, a major. Who would also have more power and authority than a private. I believe this is why the ancient gods or deities (Satan and his fallen angels) had varying degrees of power and authority. The Bible mentions the archangel Michael as being the highest-ranking angel in heaven. The answer to why these deities are no longer present in our physical world is explained in the Bible, in the book of Revelation.

Then war broke out in heaven, Michael and his angels fought against the dragon [the devil], and the dragon and his angels [demons] fought back. But they were not strong enough, and they lost their place in heaven. The great dragon was hurled down— that ancient serpent called the devil, or Satan, who leads the whole world astray. He was hurled to the earth, and his angels with him. Then I heard a loud voice in heaven say: "Now have come the salvation and the power and the kingdom of our God, and the authority of his messiah [Jesus]. For the accuser of our brothers and sisters, who accuses them before God day and night, has been hurled down." (Revelation 12:7–10)

The devil and his demons were all kicked out of heaven. According to the Bible, Jesus was there and was an eye witness to all this. Jesus, talking to his disciples, describing the devil being thrown out of heaven, said this in Luke 10:17–19, "Jesus replied, 'I saw Satan fall like lightning from heaven.'"

The reason these beings or mythological gods are not physically active in the world any longer is described in this scripture.

> And the angels who did not keep their positions of authority but abandoned their proper dwelling—these he [God], has kept in darkness, bound with everlasting chains for judgment on the great Day. (Jude 1:6)

The devil was cast out of heaven, down to earth, and is leading the whole world astray. He still has a countless number of demons that remain scattered out across the earth as a great army. They hate mankind, and their only mission is to destroy all of us. Why?

Because God loves us. They still have power and authority, according to their rank, and are using it to kill, steal from, and destroy all humanity.

The Bible says in Revelation 12:12, "Therefore, rejoice you, heavens and you who dwell in them! But woe to the earth and the sea, because the devil has gone down to you! He is filled with fury, because he knows his time is short."

The devil will do anything to take as many people (souls) with him as he can. He even masquerades as an angel of light to deceive people into thinking they have seen and talked to an angel of God. He is deceiving and destroying people and will drag as many of us to hell with him as he can. This is what the devil has been doing from the beginning and will keep on doing until the time comes for the judgment when he, his demon horde, and all those lost souls he has deceived will be thrown into the lake of fire for all eternity.

And no wonder, for Satan himself masquerades as an

angel of light. (2 Corinthians 11:14)

I believe this is what my stepfather experienced the first time he died and was revived. A deception from the devil. Masquerading as the light of God or an angel of God. Trying to make him think he was ready for death. The second time he died, I believe the devil thought he had him for all eternity and was dragging him screaming into hell. God was extremely gracious and gave him another, very rare opportunity to make things right with him, which in fact he did. He did end up passing away a few years later from lung cancer.

Many religions started from a deception of the devil, people believing in the lies the devil has tricked them into believing. He will do anything to confuse as many people as he can. Those lies whispered into the ears of people, who do not know how to distinguish the truth. The visitation from the devil or a demon posing as an angel of God, starting yet another false religion. Many churches and different religions, even in our society today, are completely off base and deceived. The devil has infiltrated many of our churches. He has deceived people with his lies and half-truths, just as he did with Eve in the garden, causing her to believe his lies, causing her and Adam to fall into sin. The devil is still at war with God and also with us. The war being waged now is for the souls of men. The devil knows the Bible better than any of us and how to twist it around to confuse people. He knows it inside and out because he has lived it. When he came to tempt Jesus in the wilderness, the devil used the Word of God to try and trick even Jesus into sinning. Jesus responded to him also using the Word of God to counter the devil's attack.

> Put on the full armor of God, so that you can take your stand against the devil's schemes. (Ephesians 6:11)

The devil will strategically place stumbling blocks in people's paths to send people, especially church leaders, down the wrong paths. If he can deceive the teachers, then the students will be deceived as well. It is very obvious that some of our nation's largest church denominations are allowing sinful, worldly practices into their churches. Practices that are absolutely not sanctioned by the Bible. These churches, started decades ago by godly men, started on the right track with a right heart and spirit. But, unfortunately, somewhere down the line, the devil got his foot in the door. He was able to deceive the leaders into allowing things into the churches that cause people to stumble. The devil has done his job well.

> But even if we or an angel from heaven should preach a gospel other than the one, we preached to you, let them be under God's curse! (Galatians 1:8)

> Son of man, these men have set up idols in their hearts and put wicked stumbling blocks before their faces.

Should I let them inquire of
me at all? (Ezekiel 14:3)

Any church or religion that does not con-
fess, believe, and teach that Jesus is the Christ,
the Son of God, the savior of the world is a
false religion and a lie straight from hell!

Who is the liar? It is whoever denies that Jesus is the
Christ. Such a person is the
antichrist—denying   the
Father and the Son. (1 John
2:22)

It is so unfortunate in the society we live
in today, you can't even mention the name of
Jesus in public without being scoffed at. Why?
Because the power of God is in the name of
Jesus, and the devil absolutely does not want
Jesus's name mentioned. You can talk about
buddha, you can talk about Mormonism,
you can talk about Muslim, Islam, reincarna-
tion, or any other religion. You can cuss, say
the f—word in public. You can talk about any
other name or topic without reproach. But

mention the name of Jesus and people completely freak out. His name can cause people to be extremely uncomfortable.

One time, my pastor was asked to come to a city council meeting and start the proceedings in prayer. They told him he could pray, but he was absolutely not to mention the name of Jesus. Why, unless it was absolute truth, would it be so frowned upon? My pastor declined to go. It would have been just going through the motions. The prayer would have had no power behind it. Again, the power of God is in the name of Jesus. Why would a name be so disdained? Why specifically would the name of Jesus not be allowed to be mentioned in schools, at work, or anywhere else without people being completely bent out of shape? Why? Because there is the spirit of the anti-Christ being pushed on the world. This is the devil hard at work trying to stifle the work God has done for us. To conceive yet another even greater deception.

To deceive the world into believing that Jesus does not exist either.

The Fall of Man

This chapter of the book is one that addresses the reason the title of the book is *You Are Already Dead*. Some of the scriptures and topics to come in the next couple chapters will very directly address some very sensitive societal topics. So please understand that no one group of people are being targeted. The scriptures being quoted are to emphasize the fallen condition of *all* mankind. Not to condemn any one specific group or person. God loves all of us more than we can possibly know but hates our sin. The Bible was not written to condemn us, but for all of us to be saved through it. So please don't stop reading before you have all the information.

Hopefully, we have established in your mind that man is more than just a physical being. Much more than something that is just here for a little while and then gone. We are, again, also a spiritual being. Inside this mortal body, we all have a spirit or soul that will live forever somewhere. This spirit is what gives life to our mortal bodies. The Bible states that when God created man, Adam and Eve, they were made in the image of God. They were created to be perfect, with a pure spirit, and without sin.

> Then God said, "Let us make mankind *in our own image, in our likeness*, so that they may rule over the fish in the sea and the birds in the sky, over the livestock and all the wild animals, and over all the creatures that move along the ground." (Genesis 1:26)

When God used the term "in our image," he is referring to himself and Jesus as being present. Both of them, along with the Holy Spirit, were there when mankind was created.

In Genesis 1:27, it says, "So God created mankind in His own image. In the image of God, He created them; Male and female He created them."

I believe he states it this way so that there is no question we were all made in God's own image. We were not made in the image of a monkey that evolved. Man was originally created to live forever. To walk in fellowship and to have a close, personal relationship with God himself. A true Father-son and Father-daughter relationship. I say a true relationship because many people in our society grew up never having had a real, close, loving relationship with their parents. Unfortunately for all of us, because of their disobedience, Adam and Eve severed that personal relationship with God. They severed it for themselves and for all mankind. After God created Adam and Eve, they were given a wonderful place to live, where God himself walked and talked with them. He protected them and took care of all their needs. He made the garden of Eden for them to live in and gave them every tree and fruit in the garden from which they could eat, except one.

Now the Lord God had planted a garden in the east, in Eden; and there he put the man [Adam] he had formed. The Lord God made all kinds of trees grow out of the ground, trees that were pleasing to the eye and good for food. In the middle of the garden was the tree of the knowledge of good and evil. (Genesis 2:8–9)

But God did say, you must not eat fruit from the tree that is in the middle of the garden [the tree of the knowledge of good and evil] and you must not touch it, or you will surely die. (Genesis 3:3)

When God said, "you will surely die," he was not talking only about physical death, because Adam and Eve were still alive physically after they ate of the fruit. God was talking about eternal, spiritual death. When Adam and Eve ate the forbidden fruit, whatever kind of fruit it may have been, they made the choice to be disobedient, they sinned against God. When they sinned against God, they allowed disobedience (sin) into their hearts, into their spirits, and into the world. It wasn't eating a cursed fruit that caused them to die spiritually. It was a willful act of disobedience against God. It was the deliberate sin that caused them to die spiritually. It changed their spiritual nature from a pure, clean spirit to a sinful spirit. This sin not only caused them to die spiritually, it also allowed all the sickness, disease, and physical death into the world. It allowed the devil free reign on the earth to do basically whatever he wanted. There was no sickness, no disease, or physical death in the world before Adam and Eve sinned. Man allowed all these things into the world, not God. God created it all to be perfect.

According to the Bible, in the book of Genesis, in the early days of mankind, men lived hundreds of years, even after sin entered into the world. For example, just to name a few the Bible mentions, Adam lived 930 years, Seth lived 807 years, Enosh lived 905 years, Kenan lived 910 years, and Lamech lived 777 years. As the Bible continues to name those who lived in the early times, their life spans start to get shorter and shorter. The reason for this, I believe, is that as man's sinfulness started to increase in the world, sickness and disease also became more prevalent as well. Because of these things, man started dying younger and younger. Also, because of this sin and disobedience, man could no longer have that same fellowship with God. Sin caused us to be eternally separated from the God who created us. God is holy and pure and cannot even look upon sin.

> There is no one Holy like the Lord; There is no one besides you; There is no rock like our God. (1 Samuel 2:2)

> Exalt the Lord our God and worship at his holy mountain, for the Lord our God is holy. (Psalm 99:9)

> This is the message we have heard from him and declare to you: God is light; in him there is no darkness at all. (1 John 1:5)

Adam was created to be the father of all mankind. When he sinned, his spirit nature changed from a pure sinless spirit to a spiritually dead, sinful nature. Now, because of that choice, everyone who has ever been born in Adam and Eve's line has a sinful nature. Our sinful nature is contrary to God's pure and holy nature. We are now at enmity with God. Our sinful nature has caused us to be in opposition to God. We are all spiritually dead and can never stand in the presence of a holy God.

> Therefore, just as sin entered the world through one man [Adam] and death through sin, and in this way, death came to all people, because all sinned. (Romans 5:12)

As for you, you were dead in your transgressions and sins, in which you used to live when you followed the ways of this world and of the ruler of the kingdom of the air [the devil], the spirit who is now at work in those who are disobedient. *All of us* also lived among them at one time, gratifying the cravings of our flesh and following its desires and thoughts. Like the rest, we were by nature deserving of wrath. (Ephesians 2:1–3)

In a similar fashion to a father passing a blood disorder or hereditary disease down through his family lineage—from father to son, from father to daughter, and so on—so, also, that sinfulness, that tainted blood, that diseased spirit, has been passed down from Adam and Eve. It has been passed through the spirit of man, through every generation, to everyone one of us.

In Psalm 51:5, the psalmist says, "Surely, I was sinful at birth, sinful from the time my mother conceived me."

It's easy to look back over the decades and see the moral decay compounding in our world. Over the last fifty or sixty years or so, it seems our morality as a society has declined at an explosive pace. In the past five to ten years or so, it seems that the whole world has gone completely crazy. It says in the Bible that sinful man will never enter heaven, and all of us are sinful. None of us, no matter how much good we think we have done.

In Romans 3:23, the Bible says, "For *all* have sinned and fall short of the glory of God."

Also, in 1 Corinthians 6:9–10, it says, "Do you not know that wrong doers [sinners] will not inherit the kingdom of God [heaven]. Do not be deceived: neither the sexually immoral nor idolaters nor adulterers nor homosexual offenders nor thieves nor the greedy nor drunkards. None of these will ever inherit the kingdom of God!"

God cannot have fellowship with sinful man. He says when talking about mankind in Psalm 14:3, "*All* have turned away, *all* have become corrupt; there is no one who does good, no not even one."

Only the righteous will enter heaven. Nothing or no one that is unclean will ever enter his holy heaven.

> Only what is pure will enter the city [heaven]. No one who causes people to believe lies will enter it. No one who does shameful things will enter it either. Only those whose names are written in the Lamb's book of life will enter the city. (Revelation 21:27)

> For I tell you that unless your righteousness surpasses that of the Pharisees and the teachers of the law, you will certainly not enter the kingdom of heaven. Pharisees and teachers of the law were

the spiritual leaders of that
time. (Matthew 5:20)

You may be saying, "I'm not a bad person. I have never hurt anyone. I don't steal. I don't cheat. I try to live a good life." Unfortunately, it's not about us being good enough or doing enough good things. The Bible says, to enter God's holy heaven, we have to be perfect.

Matthew 5:8 says, that we must be perfect, even as our Father in heaven is perfect.

How could any of us ever possibly be perfect? If we sin just one time in our lifetime, we are no longer perfect. If we were to sin just one time a day, and we all surely sin much more than that, over a life span of, say, just seventy-five years, that one sin a day totals well over 27,000 sins. That's just one sin a day. Sin has eternally separated us all from God. We are alienated from God because of our sinful state. You might be thinking to yourself, "There is no God. No one sees what goes on here. No one knows what I think or what I do." But what if you're wrong and there is an all-powerful God who sees it all? After you have chosen to live your life doing everything as you please, what are you going to say when you find yourself standing before a holy God, and he asks you, "Why should I let you into my holy heaven?"

In Hebrews 4:13, it says, "Nothing in all creation is hidden from God's sight. Everything is uncovered and laid bare before the eyes of him to whom we must give account."

> Before a word is on my tongue, you, Lord, know it completely. (Psalm 139:4)

There are those, of course, we as a society consider to be good people in this world. People who try to do what is right. Those people who try to always do good. Those who feed and clothe the poor. Those who help others who are in need. The heroes of our society. The firefighters, the police, the doctors, and the nurses. Those who even put their own lives in jeopardy to save others. Others sit in church week after week, year after year. They give their money to the church, good causes, and try to be good Christians. Surely these people deserve to go to heaven. These are all good things, and we never want to stop doing good. But according to the Bible, none of these good works can ever get anyone into heaven. We can't make ourselves good enough to enter a holy heaven. We can't do enough good things. Good deeds can never cancel out our sinfulness.

Isaiah 64:6 tells us that, "*All* have become as one who is unclean, and all our righteous acts are like filthy rags; we all shrivel up like a leaf, and like the wind our sins sweep us away."

The Bible says we have actually become enemies of God. You may be saying, "I don't really believe in God, but I don't consider myself an enemy of God." Our sinfulness, the sinful nature we have inherited, has made us enemies.

As enemies of God, there is now only a "fearful expectation of judgment and of raging fire that will consume the enemies of God" (Hebrews 10:27).

This leaves one place for sinful man (all of us) to go when we take our last breath in this world: *hell!* Hell, as described in the Bible, is a fiery pit or the lake of fire and burning sulfur. This place was created for the devil and his demons, for their eternal punishment, now also for sinful man. We will all die, and then we will all face the judgment of God.

In Hebrews 9:27, the Bible states, "It is appointed for man once to die and then the judgment."

> Then I saw a great white throne and the one who sat upon it. Nothing could stand before or against His presence, nothing in Heaven or on the earth. I saw the dead, great and small standing before the throne of God! And books were opened. Then another book was opened; THE BOOK OF LIFE! The dead were judged by what was written in the books, by the way they had lived. The sea released the dead that was in them, death and hades released

the dead that were in them. Every, man and woman, was judged by the way he or she lived, then death and hell were hurled into the lake of fire [a fiery lake of burning sulfur], to be tormented forever. This is the second death. Anyone who's name was not found written in the LAMBS BOOK OF LIFE, was also hurled into the lake of fire, to be tortured and tormented for all eternity. (Revelation 20:11–15)

The Lamb's Book of Life is the Lord's book. This book has a record of everyone who has ever accepted Jesus as their Lord and Savior. Those who will spend eternity in heaven. This passage in Revelation also tells me that everything we do in this world is being recorded in heaven, and we will all be judged accordingly. Nothing we do, say, or even think is hidden from God.

> For by your words you will
> be acquitted, and by your
> words you will be con-
> demned. (Matthew 12:37)

All these things we have been talking about is very serious stuff and can be extremely scary. This is our eternity we're talking about. We may live seventy or eighty years, or even into our nineties, in this flesh-and-blood body. But that is just a blink of an eye compared to where you will spend all eternity.

> Why, you do not even know
> what will happen tomorrow.
> What is your life? You are a
> mist that appears for a lit-
> tle while and then vanishes.
> (James 4:14)

Well, so far you have told me that I'm already dead spiritually. I am eternally separated from God. I am actually considered an enemy of God. That even the good things I try to do are considered as filthy rags before a holy God. That I and everyone else is going to be thrown into hell. Into a lake of fire to be tortured for all eternity. Wow, that's just awesome! So what's the answer for all this? How can I avoid this impending judgment? What can I do? Again, all this can be really scary when you think about all that you have just learned, but if you choose it, your story can have a much, much better ending.

Our Degraded Society

O̲ur society has fallen a great distance morally from where we once were. As a nation, we at one time had our foundational beliefs in God and his Word (the Bible). Our country was founded on godly, biblical principles. From the very beginning, when God established the world and created man, he gave us moral absolutes to live by. He gave us the Ten Commandments first and then gave us the Bible as a guide for the way we should conduct ourselves. When God gave these moral absolutes for mankind to live by, he was not trying to restrict us or keep us from having fun. He was trying to protect us from the eternal consequences of our immoral actions.

Unfortunately, a great majority, of our society is not governed by moral absolutes anymore. So many people in our society don't seem to have any moral compass at all. We try to live our lives in the gray areas, some just blatantly evil. We try to justify our immoral actions with attitudes like, "Well, if it doesn't hurt anyone else, then it must be okay." "What I do in my own home is none of your business." Or "If I don't get caught, then I must have gotten away with it." "It was the cashier's fault, she gave me too much change, so I'm keeping it." Or "No one saw us back into that other car, let's get out of here." So many not taking responsibility for their own actions. Not caring about how our actions affect other people. What people don't seem to realize is there are consequences for every action, right and wrong. There are eternal consequences for every individual and for our society. Our immoral personal choices actually do adversely affect our society as a whole. Whether we choose to believe it or not, the way we live our lives is our choice. Whether it be conscious or subconscious, our morality or immorality comes down to our own personal choices. We may blame our behavior on our mothers, or on the way we were treated by our fathers, or even on the pressures of society. But in the end, we will all be judged on our own merits, on our own choices.

We were once considered a Christian nation. I don't think any country in the world could consider us a Christian nation anymore. A great deal of our society, I believe, doesn't even care to be categorized as a Christian nation. We have taken the Bible and prayer out of our schools. Out of our court rooms. Out of virtually every government building. The signs and plaques that proudly displayed the Ten Commandments, those that have been in these buildings for decades, are forcibly removed. I heard a government official giving the pledge of allegiance at a political function on television recently. When it came time to recite the part about being one nation under God, she completely left it out. She substituted something totally different in its place. Men are literally trying to take God out of our society as a whole. How can God bless a nation that has turned its back on him? Our immorality has and will inhibit God from working in our lives and blessing us personally and as a nation. Why do you think there is so much chaos in our country and in our world?

Even the mentioning of the name Jesus in our schools, government buildings, and in places of business can get you harassed or even fired. How is it even possible that simply mentioning the name of Jesus can make people so uncomfortable? How can something that represents and promotes only love, compassion, goodness, integrity, righteousness, purity, morality, good conduct, obedience to the authorities, grace, mercy, hope, and forgiveness? How can these things that represent only good be considered to be a bad thing? How can a nation turn so quickly from what we were founded upon to what we as a nation have become? A sinful, selfish, self-centered, self-absorbed, ungodly, disobedient, sexually perverted nation. The reason is, there is the spirit of the anti-Christ working practically uninhibited. The devil is working so strongly in this nation and in the world that we have literally turned upside down morally.

Our ancestors would turn over in their graves if they could see what we as a nation and a world have become. Our prisons are overflowing with men and women sent there for grievous acts on their fellow man. Murder, rape, robbery, drugs, and sexual depravity has become so prevalent in our society. We can't take our eyes off our babies, even for a moment, or some perverted psycho may rape and kill them. Evil is very present in our society, and we have become so desensitized to it, it has now become the norm. We have become, I believe, one of the most immoral nations in the world. We have become so evil, in some other countries' eyes, they refer to the US as the great Satan. This entire world is in utter turmoil. Our kids are walking into their schools and killing each other. Drugs are an epidemic. Suicide, especially in our teens, is at all-time highs. Our economy is in shambles. Wars and natural disasters are everywhere and getting more frequent.

There have been cities and entire countries toppled because of the same types of sinfulness, disobedience, and sexual depravity we have allowed into our own society. Cities that were utterly destroyed because of their wickedness. The Bible documents several cities and nations that, when judgment came upon them, were completely destroyed. The cities of Sodom and Gomorrah, just to name two, were destroyed because of their sin, sexual immorality and debauchery. Fire and burning sulfur literally rained down from heaven and utterly destroyed them. The Bible talks about this in Jude 7: In a similar manner, Sodom and Gomorrah and the surrounding towns gave themselves up to sexual immorality and perversion. They serve as an example of those who suffer the punishment of eternal fire.

There are absolutely catastrophic consequences for the sinfulness we have allowed into our lives, our country, and our world. What hope is there for a future in a world that is taking the only real hope we have and tossing it aside? When you take God out of society, you take true hope out of society. Why again do you think the suicide rate and drug overdoses are at epidemic levels in our teens? A couple years ago, I was at my granddaughter's high school for one of her school functions. I noticed a large wall full of pictures and the names of students. I asked her if she was on it, thinking it was for honor students or something of that nature. She then went on to tell me it was a memorial wall for the students at the school who had died. Most were from suicide, drug overdoses, and drunk driving accidents. I was literally shocked at the number of pictures. This was a very large wall.

If our kids are led to believe this dark, evil world is all there is, telling them they are only here for a little while and then just gone, if they are led to believe there are no eternal rewards or eternal consequences for their actions, it would completely explain why they have been left with the hopeless attitudes that so many of them have. Attitudes like, "Why should I even bother? Why should I keep on trying? Why shouldn't I just give up? Why shouldn't I just do anything that feels good? Why should I keep on hurting? Why not just kill myself and get it over with?" This train of thought is, unfortunately, becoming more and more prevalent in our teens.

Proverbs 13:12 says, "Hope deferred makes the heart sick, but a longing fulfilled is a tree of life."

Suicide is now the second leading cause of death in our kids from the ages of ten to twenty-four years. Young people, I am here to tell you that God has an awesome plan for your life. He will fill you with a hope and a peace that nothing else in this world can give you if you let him.

> "For I know the plans I have for you," declares the Lord, "plans to prosper you and not to harm you, plans to give you hope and a future." (Jeremiah 29:11)

My oldest grandson, who went to the same high school, has unfortunately had to see this firsthand in his own personal peer group. In the span of just a few short years, from high school to young adulthood, he has had, I believe, six or seven close friends, and a sister, die from suicide and drug overdoses. This is a travesty that should never be. Our kids are looking for anything to fill that emptiness, that hopelessness, and to deaden the intense pain they feel inside. There is only one thing that can fill this void. The one thing that our society is taking away from them:

Jesus. He is the only real, tested, and proven hope we have in this world.

> May the God of hope fill
> you with all joy and peace as
> you trust in him, so that you
> may overflow with hope by
> the power of the Holy Spirit.
> (Romans 15:13)

These young tragedies are, unfortunately, just some of the consequences reaped by a sinful, non-God-fearing society. I truly believe most people in our society are just trying to make it through this life to the best of their ability. They make choices and decisions based on what they know. On what they have seen and been taught by previous generations. The problem with this is our society is teaching them that we don't need God. Teaching them that our sinful, selfish, ungodly, worldly way of doing things is acceptable. As we teach our children the ways of the world, our sinfulness as a society grows at an exponential rate. The next generation ends up more sinful, immoral, more ungodly, and feeling more hopeless than the last. I believe most people don't even think many of the things they participate in are wrong. Why? Because these immoral actions are now so accepted in our society as being normal. Just because something is deemed acceptable by society or even legalized by our leaders, does not make them moral. In the eyes of a pure, holy, and righteous God, our sinful actions are utterly detestable. The Bible tells us that God loves us immensely but hates our sin.

Our servicemen in recent years have seen horrific things in battle in Iraq, the desert storm war, and other places of conflict. So many of these men and women have come home and have not been able to productively rejoin society after all they have seen and had to do. They are committing suicide at an alarming rate as well. In many cases, also killing their wives and children along with them. This just recently happened to one of my daughter's best friends. Her husband was a veteran of the war in Iraq. He was suffering intensely from PTSD. Because of the hope-lessness he felt, one night, he spiraled out of control, shot and killed her, then took his own life, leaving three beautiful babies without their mommy and daddy.

This is a dramatic difference from our servicemen who fought in earlier wars, for instance, world war one and two. Many more of these men and women came back home and were able to live happy, productive lives. The suicide rate was much lower even though they were exposed to the same types of horrific things. I believe the reason for the dramatic difference in the state of mental health between these two groups of veterans was that in the earlier wars, we, as a society, and these men and women, were much more grounded in God's Word (the Bible). Many more of them were raised up from childhood to trust in God and godly principles. Many more of them had a foundation of hope for their futures and hope for a heavenly eternity.

In our society today, the same things that were thought to be sinful and wrong in that era are now somehow accepted by society, as though they are the norm and not considered to be wrong anymore. The good, wholesome, and godly things now are thought to be the unaccepted and the taboo. Not very many years ago, the girl who had sex before she was married was considered by her peers to be a whore and the outcast. Now, if a girl makes it through high school and is still a virgin, she is the oddball. Getting pregnant as a high school student is now extremely common. Many schools even have daycare facilities operating in them because there are so many unwed teenage mothers. I have even heard stories of young teenage girls subjected to teasing and ridicule from her peers because she chose not to have sex. Because she made the moral choice to save herself for marriage. How did we, as a society, do a complete moral flip flop? How did morality and godliness become the wrong thing to do? God is not the one who changed, we did! The bible says in Hebrews 13:8, "Jesus Christ is the same yesterday and today and forever."

Also, in Psalm 55:19, "God, who is enthroned from of old, *who does not change—* he will hear them and humble them, because they have no fear of God."

The Bible actually foretold (prophesied) these times. It says, in the end times, that good would be spoken of as evil and evil would be spoken of as good.

Isaiah 5:20 says, "Woe to those who call evil good and good evil, who put darkness for light and light for darkness, who put bitter for sweet and sweet for bitter."

This is exactly what is happening in our world today. It's like a mirror image of what the Bible says it was like in the days of Noah when the flood came that covered the whole earth and destroyed all mankind. I'm sure you have heard the Bible story of Noah and the ark. Noah was the only man in the entire world God found to be righteous and blameless in his sight. That's why God chose to save Noah and his family. For the skeptic, there is actual archeological evidence that the earth was flooded at one time.

> This is the account of Noah and his family. Noah was a righteous man, blameless among the people of his time, and he walked faithfully with God. (Genesis 6:9)

Genesis 6:5 says that, in the days of Noah, the sinfulness and wickedness of man was great, that every inclination of man's hearts were evil.

Man's sin and sexual depravity had become so great that man had become depraved.

> The earth was corrupted in God's sight and filled with violence, all flesh had corrupted their way. Their hearts were hardened, their ears were dulled to the things and to the voice of God. No one repented of their sin, and no one cared to seek God their creator. (Genesis 6:11–12)

Second Timothy 3:1–4 describes our end time society this way: "But mark this: There will be terrible times in the last days. People will be lovers of themselves, lovers of money, boastful, proud, abusive, disobedient to their parents, ungrateful, unholy, without love, unforgiving, slanderous, without self-control, brutal, not lovers of the good, treacherous, rash, conceited, lovers of pleasure rather than lovers of God!"

Does this not describe exactly the society in which we are currently living? When Jesus describes the end times and the events that surround his second coming, he says in Luke 17:26, "Just as it was in the days of Noah, so it will be in the days of the Son of Man. People were eating and drinking, marrying and being given in marriage, until the day Noah entered the ark, the flood came and destroyed them all."

> By that same word the present heavens and earth are reserved for fire, being kept for the day of judgment and destruction of the ungodly. (2 Peter 3:7)

People were living their lives doing anything and everything that felt good, ignoring Noah's warnings and pleas to save themselves. They thought Noah was crazy. Some crazy guy building a giant ship on dry land in the middle of nowhere. And to make it worse, up until that time, it had never rained. The people disregarded God and his impending judgment on the world, and they were all destroyed. They took God, their creator, out of society and suffered the consequences. Now, we, as a society, are doing exactly the same things they did in Noah's time. Some things we have allowed into our own society are even much worse. We have become so perverted as a society, so deceived by the devil, that even abortion, the killing of our babies in the womb, all to the god of convenience, has become such an accepted practice in our society. Many people consider it to be just another minor medical procedure.

The doctors and our society are leading these young women to believe they are just removing a lump of tissue. How is it possible that anyone could ever think that killing an innocent baby at any stage of development could ever be okay? If you are naive enough to believe these tiny babies are just a lump of tissue and not a little life, you have obviously never seen the pictures I have seen of these little aborted babies. Pictures of those tiny little dismembered bodies. Those precious little babies who had tiny little arms, legs, fingers, and toes. Some so-called doctor literally ripped apart in its mother's womb. Whatever happened to morality? What happened to the Hippocratic oath these doctors took to do no harm? Abortion to them is not about helping young women or being a woman's choice. With these groups, it all comes down to the money they make, by performing these atrocities. The Bible tells us that God himself is the one who forms us in our mother's womb. God says in his Word that he knew us before we were ever born. That he had all our day's numbered before one of them ever came to be.

Jeremiah 1:5 says, "Before I formed you in the womb, I knew you, before you were born, I set you apart."

If you are one of those unfortunate ones who have fallen into this trap, one of the many deceived by the devil and have had an abortion, know that God is a forgiving God. He still loves you immeasurably! There is forgiveness and redemption in Christ Jesus.

There are also so many ungodly and immoral sexual practices now literally being pushed on to our society. Sexual immorality, perversion, and debauchery is everywhere. It is all over the television, in movies, and now even in most media. Now these immoral practices have become so accepted in our society, they are becoming the social norm. Just a few years ago, these practices were completely unacceptable and considered to be detestable by our society. Now, if anyone were to dare to speak negatively about or be in opposition to these practices, they are considered to be not politically correct and subject to ridicule, possibly even retribution. Actors and actresses also prostituting themselves to millions for fame and fortune. Just thirty or forty years ago, some of the same scenes you can now see on regular television were then considered to be pornography. Our society has been completely desensitized to what is actually immoral. All of these so-called sexual freedoms we have allowed into our society will ultimately bring judgment on us. Just as the cities of Sodom and Gomorrah came under judgment for their immorality and were destroyed. I believe we as a society are on the same track. It may not rain down fire and brimstone from heaven, but judgment nonetheless. The Bible says in 1 Corinthians 6:18, "Flee from sexual immorality. All other sins a person commits are outside the body, but whoever sins sexually, sins against their own body."

There are spirits, evil spirits, at work in this country and the world. They have very successfully undermined and now even blatantly continue to undermine the very moral fabric of our society. They are perverting the minds and hearts of people. These are all signs of a society that has become sinful, immoral, demoralized, and depraved. Just as it was in the days of Noah. All our personal and immoral choices do absolutely negatively affect our society as a whole. The Bible, again, does not condemn these practices to restrict us. God is also not condemning us as a person. He is condemning the sinfulness in us. He condemns these sinful practices because he knows they are absolutely detrimental to us, personally and as a society. They will eventually consume and destroy us. We are a generation deceived by the devil. Deceived into believing the immorality we have allowed into our lives and our society is okay.

How do you tell a world the things they are participating in and the way they are living is evil? How do you tell them and do it with love, grace, and compassion? Especially when most don't even think what they are doing is wrong?

> Jesus said, "The world hates me because I testify that its works are evil." (John 7:7)

> If the world hates you, keep in mind that it hated me first. (John 15:18)

There are absolutely catastrophic consequences for the immorality we have allowed into our lives, both personally and corporately. I believe we as a society are already reaping many of those consequences. Judgment has already come upon us in so many ways: that memorial wall at my grandchildren's school of all those dead children, my grandson's sister and all his friends, deceived into thinking death was their only way out. These are just a small portion of the consequences our society has already reaped. In my experience, when someone commits suicide. It not only destroys the person who took their own life. The devil will also try to use it to multiply the hopelessness in those around them as well. That one act of desperation has a huge negative impact on the parents, siblings, or on the children who are left behind. Even in that individual's peer group, one suicide often leads to others committing the same desperate act. You can't take God out of society and still expect to have hope. You can't take God out of society and expect to have order. God has made himself visible in everything he has created, but we seem to be completely blind to him.

It says in Romans1:20, "For since the creation of the world God's invisible qualities—his eternal power and divine nature—have been clearly seen, being understood from what has been made, so that people are without excuse."

I have listened attentively, but they do not say what is right. None of them repent of their wickedness, saying, "What have I done?" Each pursues their own course like a horse charging into battle. (Jeremiah 8:6)

This nation has been sewing a lot of bad mojo for a long time. How can we not reap the consequences of what we have been doing? As I mentioned earlier, I believe our society and our world is already reaping some of the consequences of what we have been sowing. Some people call this karma. We are going to get back what we have been giving. This is actually a biblical principle. The Bible calls this the principle of sowing and reaping. In the same manner that a farmer sows a little seed and reaps a whole field of produce, according to the Bible, we will reap what we sow. We will reap more than we sow, later than we sow. We will reap individually and as a society.

> Do not be deceived: God cannot be mocked. A man reaps what he sows, whoever sows to please their flesh, from the flesh will reap destruction; whoever sows to please the Spirit [God], from the Spirit will reap eternal life. (Galatians 6:7–8)

The principle is if we sow good things, then we will reap good things. If we sow bad, we will reap bad. Sometimes though, we see immoral and even downright ungodly people who seem to prosper in everything they do. They seem to have no problems and no worries. They seem to have it all, according to what our society attributes to having it all. The big house, the really expensive cars, good health, the most attractive spouse, and more money than they could ever spend. All with the unquenchable desire for more. They seem to be reaping good, even though it's very evident they have sown a lot of bad seed.

There was a scene from an awesome Christian movie that aired a couple years ago, which addresses this issue very directly. The son in the movie was a very successful and very uncaring businessman. His mother was a godly woman who was suffering from an illness like Alzheimer's or dementia. She had no recollection of who he was. She did not remember her own name and just sat staring into nothingness. In the scene, he is in the room with her, asking the question "Why should I believe in God? Everything in my life is great. I have good health. I have no problems, no worries, and I have the best of everything. On the contrary you have lived for God all your life. You have nothing to show for it. You're in a nursing home, and look at you, you can't even remember your own name."

Suddenly, she perks up and replies through the Holy Spirit, completely to his disbelief. She says to him, "Sometimes the devil allows people to live a life free from trouble, because he doesn't want them turning to God. Sin is like a jail cell you've accepted. It's so comfy, you don't see any need to leave. The door is wide open, but you choose to stay. But one day time runs out, that cell door slams shut, and suddenly it's too late." This life is going to come to an end, and then, they as well as all of us will face the judgment. They may have seemed to reap good in this life in spite of how they lived. But they may have also traded having it all in the world for eternal judgment and an eternity in hell. Reaping now, their true reward or, more accurately, the consequences for how they lived.

> What good is it for someone to gain the whole world, yet forfeit their soul? Or what will someone give in exchange for their soul? (Matthew 16:26)

> Again I tell you it is easier for a camel to go through the eye of a needle than for someone who is rich to enter the kingdom of God. (Matthew 19:24)

The Bible addresses this topic as well in the book of Psalms. The godly man who wrote this psalm was distressed that the sinful, ungodly people seemed to always prosper, but the godly seemed to be the ones always distressed. Until he realized in the end, they would reap eternal consequences at the final judgment.

> This is what the wicked are like—always carefree, they go on amassing wealth. Surely in vain I have kept my heart pure and have washed my hands in innocence. All day long I have been afflicted, and every morning brings new punishments. If I had spoken out like that, I would have betrayed your children. When I tried to understand all this, it troubled me deeply till I entered the sanctuary of God; then I understood their final destiny. Surely you place them on slippery ground; you cast them down to ruin. How

suddenly are they destroyed,
completely swept away by
terrors! (Psalm 73:12–19)

You may be thinking, "I don't believe in all that garbage, it all sounds like nonsense to me." Let me say this. Just because you don't believe in something, doesn't mean it does not exist. You can say, "I don't believe in the wind because I have never seen it," but it still exists. If you are looking, you can see the evidence of the wind. The trees swaying back and forth. The grass being bent over from it. The clouds moving across the sky. In the same manner, if you are truly looking for it, there is evidence of all the things I have been talking about as well. We will reap what we sow. We will reap more than we sow, later than we sow. The Bible is very clear that when we die, we will all face our eternal judgment, determining where we will spend eternity. We will all stand before a Holy and Just God, individually, and give an account for our lives.

Romans 14:11 says, "It is written: 'As surely as I live,' says the Lord, 'every knee will bow before me; every tongue will acknowledge God.'"

Also, in Hebrews 9:27, it says, "It is appointed once for man to die, and then to face the judgment."

Do we dare face this eternal judgment without turning from our immoral ways? Without accepting the forgiveness that is offered by God, through his son Jesus Christ? Jesus was not considered politically correct in his day either. He calls sin what it really is: sin! Again, all this being said, Jesus did not come into this world to condemn us. Our sinfulness is being brought to light because he knows that our sinful actions will ultimately destroy us. He hates our sin but loves each one of us immeasurably. He does not want us to be condemned to an eternity in hell. He gave his very life to save us from that horrible outcome.

> For God did not send his Son into the world to condemn the world, but to save the world through him. (John 3:17)

In John chapter 8, it tells this story that hopefully will give you an idea of what God's true attitude is toward us. When the people brought to Jesus a woman who was caught in the very act of adultery, which then was a sin punishable by being stoned to death, which the crowd had every intention of doing to her, Jesus defuses the crowd by saying to them, "Whoever of you is without sin, you be the first to cast a stone at her." As the crowd started dropping their stones and walking away in shame, Jesus simply looks at her in love and, with compassion, says to her, "I do not condemn you, but go and leave your life of sin."

Just as Jesus says to the woman caught in the act of adultery, he also says to you: you are loved by God more than you can ever know. He says, "I do not condemn you, but go and leave your life of sin."

> "Repent and be baptized, every one of you, in the name of Jesus Christ for the forgiveness of your sins. And you will receive the gift of the Holy Spirit. This prom-

ise is for you and your children and for all who are far off—for all whom the Lord our God will call." With many other words he warned them; and he pleaded with them, "Save yourselves from this corrupt generation." (Acts 2:38–40)

Salvation is found in no one else, for there is no other name under heaven given to mankind *by which we must be saved* [the name of Jesus]. (Acts 4:12)

With those same words, I also plead with you to save yourself! Don't wait until it's too late. Don't wait until the grim reaper comes knocking. You have the opportunity now while you are still living, while you still have breath in your lungs, to make that choice. Repent and turn your life over to the only savior of your soul, Christ Jesus. He will give you that lost hope. The hope this world is so good at taking away. Hope for the rest of your life and a sure hope for the rest of your eternity.

The Proof

From the beginning of the human race, men of every generation, in every corner of the world, men of every race, color, and creed acknowledge or believe there is a god in some form or another. Some supernatural being who created all of heaven and earth. An immortal being with unlimited power and authority, the one who created all life in the world. A supernatural being who lives in the spirit and has all power over all the earth, mankind, the angels, and all spirit beings. Out of these many beliefs, through the generations, many very diverse religions have come and gone. A few have survived for thousands of years.

Some again believe when they die, their spirit, that part of us that lives on, goes on to a higher plain to become something greater than they were in this life. Some believe they will be reincarnated, that somehow, they will come back to live another life. They get to do it all over and over again until they get it right. Or maybe they will come back as some form of animal, maybe a cow or a horse, etc. There are religions out there that believe man's spirit just floats off and becomes part of the cosmos. Some believe if they work hard enough and are good enough, they will go to heaven, whatever they believe that to be. I, even in my own sphere of influence, have family and friends who don't believe in God. They don't believe there is a heaven or a hell. They believe that when they die, they are just gone; they cease to exist.

Most people don't even want to think about death. Death to many of us is a very, very scary subject. We all, at some point in our lives though, will have to deal with it. We will all at some point have someone we know or have someone close to us die. We will all have to face death, at least temporarily. Many will drink themselves into a stupor to ease some of the pain and fear. Then they will put it behind them as quickly as they can. Many people when they are forced to face death, those without some kind of strong belief system, don't really know how to respond. When they do have someone close to them die, they may say in some unsubstantiated hope for their loved one, "Oh, they went to a better place." People don't want to even think about the possibility that someone they love could possibly go to a place like hell! They, as we all would, want them to be at rest and at peace. In reality though, they just don't really know.

Most religions, or at least a lot of them, do again believe in God, or a god, as we have already discussed. Most do also believe in some form of heaven, a beautiful, peaceful, awesome place. Which would be that better place people hope to go and hope for their loved ones. On the flip side, most do also believe in some form of hell. A place of eternal fire, judgment, torment, and utter horror. A great many religions teach that if you're good enough and you work hard enough, you might be able to work your way into heaven. And all the bad people, the sinners, the murderers, the rapists, drug dealers, thieves, and child molesters, they go to hell. The problem with that type of belief system is, it's all again based on speculation, on pure conjecture. Who decides if you're good enough? Who decides if you have sinned too much? Who decides what is actually a sin?

Think really hard about what I'm about to say. Our life on this earth is very short. We are, again, not guaranteed to be alive five minutes from now. We are also talking about where we will spend all eternity. There are a lot of views out there about what might happen after death. But what are they really basing these beliefs on? What actual proof do you have that what you believe is the truth? Do you really want to just speculate on where you will spend all your eternity? We might as well just roll the dice and hope for a positive outcome. You might be saying there is no way anyone can know for certain what really happens after death. But I would say to you, there is a way to know for certain. It has been proven time and time again. Proven in multitudes of people's lives, over several thousand years, and is absolute reality. Wouldn't it be an awesome relief to know for certain what will happen to you after you die? To actually make the choice where you will spend all of eternity. How would that knowledge change the way you live your life? How much freedom would that knowledge give to you and your family? Not to have to live your life in the fear and uncertainty of what may happen to you even if you were to die today.

There is proof that what I am saying is the truth, and it may be closer than you think. There is documentation that dates back thousands of years. Documentation that was written down by many different men over thousands of years. Men who were born in different eras. Men born hundreds and even thousands of years apart, but spoke and wrote about the same things, in the same spirit. Speaking about things foretold by others thousands of years earlier. Things that were working powerfully in their time and are still working in multitudes of people's lives today. Still working because they are reality and the only tested and proven truth man has ever had. How is it possible something that was working thousands of years ago can still be relevant for me today? Because it is the unchanging, infallible word of God. Yes, we are talking about the Bible.

You probably have one sitting in your house somewhere. It's more than likely on a dusty bookshelf or sitting somewhere with a pile of old magazines or laundry thrown on top of it. It most likely hasn't been opened in years, if ever. Why would we not want to open and read one of the oldest documents ever recorded? A book that has changed countless lives. Why? There are several reasons why we may hesitate to read it. I believe the most pre-dominant reason, though, is because of our shame. Because of fear that our deeds will be exposed. The Bible is the infallible, unchanging Word of God and is absolute truth. It's the light that brings our darkness into the light.

> Everyone who does evil hates
> the light and will not come
> into the light for fear that
> their deeds will be exposed.
> (John 3:20)

There, again, is a devil out there, and he absolutely does not want people reading the Word of God. Why? Because he knows that there is life-changing, eternal, life-saving power in those words. The Bible says in 2 Corinthians 4:4, "The god of this age [the devil], has blinded the minds of unbelievers, so that they cannot see the light of the gospel that displays the glory of Christ, who is the image of God."

The light of God's glory is revealed to us through the scriptures. The best way for us to truly know the Bible is true is to actually read it. The more we read it, the more the scriptures reveal to us the glory of God. Through them, he also confirms to our spirits that they are the true Word of God.

> For the word of God is alive and active. Sharper than any double-edged sword, it penetrates even to dividing soul and spirit, joints and marrow; it judges the thoughts and attitudes of the heart. (Hebrews 4:12)

God has breathed life into all scripture. It is useful for teaching us what is true. It is useful for correcting our mistakes. It is useful for making our lives whole again. It is useful for training us to do what is right. (2 Timothy 3:16)

There are also more tangible ways to prove to the skeptic that the Bible is real and true. For instance, the Bible proves itself through the many, many prophecies foretold and fulfilled. Well over 2,000, in fact, and most of them have been fulfilled to the smallest detail. The Bible tells us the true purpose for prophecy.

In 2 Peter 1:19, after the apostle Peter testified that he had seen Jesus Christ in all His glory, he said, "And so we have *the prophetic word* made more sure, to which you do well to pay attention as to a lamp shining in a dark place, until the day dawns and the morning star arises in our hearts."

Peter is stating that fulfilled prophecy is a witness that the scriptures are real and true.

In Isaiah 48:3 and 5, talking about prophecies, God said, "I declared the former things long ago and they went forth from My mouth, and I proclaimed them. Suddenly I acted, and they came to pass… Therefore, I declared them to you long ago, before they took place. I proclaimed them to you, lest you should say, 'My idol has done them and my, graven image and my molten image have commanded them.'"

This is God saying, "I told you all these things were going to happen, long before they came to be. This way there would be no question as to who did it." There are, again, well over 2,000 prophecies in the Bible and all but a couple hundred have been fulfilled to the tiniest detail. If you were to look up the mathematical probability that even two or three of these prophecies would be fulfilled, the odds against it are staggering. It is literally impossible that even five to ten of the prophecies in the Bible could be fulfilled. Unless, of course, something supernatural was involved. The Bible says, in 2 Peter 1:20–21, "Above all, you must understand that no prophecy of Scripture came about by the prophet's own interpretation of things. For prophecy never had its origin in the human will, but prophets, though human, spoke from God as they were carried along by the Holy Spirit."

Here are just a few of the prophecies that have been foretold and fulfilled.

Jeremiah 25:11–12, speaking about the land of Israel, says, "This whole country will become a desolate wasteland, and these nations will serve the king of Babylon seventy years. But when the seventy years are fulfilled, I will punish the king of Babylon and his nation, the land of the Babylonians, for their guilt," declares the Lord, "and will make it desolate forever." This prophecy was fulfilled by 539 BC, approximately fifty years after it was foretold.

In Jeremiah 32:36–37, he prophesies approximately fifty years before that the Jews would survive their seventy-year captivity in Babylon and return to their homeland.

In Nehemiah 2:5–6, he prophesies at least twenty years before that the city of Jerusalem would be rebuilt. But this also coincides with prophecy that gives the exact timeline of the coming of Jesus, prophesied over four hundred years earlier. It was prophesied hundreds of years earlier that Jesus would be born of a virgin.

> Therefore the Lord himself will give you a sign: The virgin [Mary] will conceive and give birth to a son, and will call him Immanuel. (Isaiah 7:14)

> The angel answered, "The Holy Spirit will come on you, and the power of the Most-High will overshadow you. So, the holy one to be born will be called the Son of God." (Luke 1:35)

It was prophesied that the Christ (Jesus) would be born in the town of Bethlehem.

> After Jesus was born in Bethlehem in Judea, during

YOU ARE ALREADY DEAD

> the time of King Herod,
> Magi [kings] from the
> east came to Jerusalem.
> (Matthew 2:1)

It was prophesied that John the Baptist would be sent ahead of Jesus to prepare the way.

Isaiah 40:3 says that John is to clear the way for the messiah (Jesus).

In Malachi 3:1, it is God who says that "he will clear the way before Me."

> But this is how God fulfilled
> what He foretold through
> all the prophets, saying that
> His Christ would suffer.
> (Acts 3:18)

Even Jesus himself prophesied that he would be crucified on a cross. When he talks about being lifted up in the next scripture, this terminology in that era was talking about being crucified.

> So Jesus said, "When you
> have lifted up the Son of
> Man, then you will know
> that I am he and that I do
> nothing on my own but
> speak just what the Father
> has taught me." (John 8:28)

God has even worked out very specific timelines that coincide with these prophecies, which makes them even more improbable. Many of the prophecies foretold the coming of Jesus. They came to pass exactly when and the way they were foretold. Paul, one of God's apostles, a man whom Jesus appeared to after he had been crucified and had risen from the dead, the author of a great majority of the New Testament, talking about the prophetical word, wrote in Romans 1:1–2, "Paul a servant of Christ Jesus, called to be an apostle and set apart for the gospel of God, the gospel he promised beforehand through his prophets in the Holy Scriptures, regarding his Son."

You may bring up the fact that other men have, in the past, had some prophetical writings come true as well. One, for instance, is Nostradamus. He wrote a book in which some of the things he wrote about came to pass with some accuracy. *Wikipedia* had this to say about Nostradamus's writings: his prophetical writings, first of all, came about by using astrology and divining. It states that most academic sources reject the fact that Nostradamus had any genuine supernatural prophetic abilities. That the associations made between world events and Nostradamus's predictions are the result of misinterpretations or misrepresentations, some deliberate.

These academics argue that Nostradamus's predictions are vague. Meaning that they could be applied to virtually anything with a little help. With that being said, I do believe that he and others absolutely could have some prophetical accuracy. But it does not come from God. Those people who are involved in astrology, divining, and fortune-telling, even if they are not aware of it, are getting their information from demons, also referred to as familiar spirits. They whisper things into the ears of people who have been deceived by the devil. Those who cannot distinguish the lies of the devil from God's truth. Demons have been around since the beginning and do have power according to their ranking and do have knowledge.

In a similar manner to God speaking prophecies and the scriptures to godly men, who then wrote them down, the devil and his horde of demons try to imitate God and do the same things to some degree. They do the latter to confuse and deceive man. The devil is a master of deception and confusion. This is what the Bible has to say about people who use these means of consorting with demons.

> I will set my face against anyone who turns to mediums and spiritists to prostitute themselves by following them, and I will cut them off from their people. (Leviticus 20:6)

> A man or woman who is a medium or spiritist among you must be put to death. You are to stone them; their

blood will be on their own
heads. (Leviticus 20:27)

God did not want demonic influence
polluting the hearts and minds of his people. I saw someone on TV just last night who
claimed to be talking to the dead relatives of
the people in the audience, with a great deal
of accuracy. These people are looking for anything to give them some kind of hope but,
to their own detriment, are seeking it in the
wrong places. The devil has deceived them
into believing that his lies are the truth.

Investigate for yourself, dig deeper into
these things. Read the Bible; as you do, God
will reveal these things to you and so much
more. Why would you not research it and see
the proof for yourself? Even archeological dis-
coveries are proving that cities, government
officials, people, and places written about in
the Bible, that many historians and scholars
thought to be mythical names and places, are
actually, historically accurate. These discover-
ies, I believe, give the Bible even more validity. The sciences have even proven many of
the topics the Bible talks about are a reality

as well. True, observational science actually proves the existence of God. It proves that all life had to begin by intelligent design. It is scientifically impossible for life to just jump or explode into existence.

I heard an interview with a very outspoken atheist scientist. In this interview, he was asked to name just one time that life ever created itself. He was at a complete loss for words. The question literally dumbfounded him, and he could not come up with an answer. A few years later, in another interview, he changed his big bang theory to the theory that the earth must have been seeded by aliens. Why is it, people can believe that life on earth could have been started by aliens, but cannot fathom the thought that an all-powerful God could have created it?

> For the wisdom of this world
> is foolishness in God's sight.
> As it is written, he catches
> the wise in their craftiness
> and again, The Lord knows
> that the thoughts of the wise

are futile. (1 Corinthians 3:19)

As intelligent as these intellects may be in the wisdom of man, they think the Word of God to be foolishness. Why? Because they are trying to discern spiritual things with limited human mental capacity.

> The person without the Spirit does not accept the things that come from the Spirit of God but considers them foolishness and cannot understand them because they are discerned only through the Spirit. (1 Corinthians 2:14)

> But we preach Christ crucified: a stumbling block to Jews and foolishness to Gentiles. (1 Corinthians 1:23)

Whether it was with a big bang or through another process, God created it all.

The Bible tells us God created the heavens and the earth in six days and on the seventh day he rested. You might be thinking, "Yeah right, God created everything in six days, that can happen." What we need to understand is the Bible says, with God, a day is like a thousand years and a thousand years are like a day.

> A thousand years in your sight are like a day that has just gone by, or like a watch in the night. (Psalm 90:4)

All these things man is trying to figure out in his own wisdom is already written down and explained for us in the Bible. It's all in there, but people refuse to believe it. Some things will remain a mystery until we meet the Lord face-to-face. He has told us everything he wants us to know now in the Bible.

> As the heavens are higher than the earth, so are my ways higher than your ways

and my thoughts than your thoughts. (Isaiah 55:9)

The fear of the Lord is the beginning of knowledge, but fools despise wisdom and instruction. (Proverbs 1:7)

There is, again, the elusive devil who blinds the hearts and minds of people, so they cannot understand the truth. The Bible is the Word of God and is absolute truth. As a Christian, God also gives us, his children, understanding through the Holy Spirit. His Spirit resides in us to give us understanding and discernment of the Bible and of spiritual things, things that man with a sinful nature cannot.

We know also that the Son of God has come and has given us understanding, so that we may know him who is true. And we are in him who is true by being in his

Son Jesus Christ. He is the
true God and eternal life. (1
John 5:20)

Atheists are the ones who are actually
living with a blind faith. Why do I say this?
Because the scientific evidence does not sup-
port or confirm their faith. All they are believing in is based on speculation and theories.
If you take time to research it, even through
man's science, what biochemistry has actually proven is, just as it says in Genesis, the
very first chapter of the Bible, in the very first
verse, it says, "In the beginning, God created
the heavens and the earth!" It can't be stated
any clearer than that! Man has been in search
of the truth about creation for thousands of
years. They have come up with many theories
and speculations of how things really began
and how they think things really work. The
reason they are called theories is because that's
all they are. Someone had an idea, or a theory,
that they have tried to prove but have never
been able to, definitively (i.e., the theory of
evolution or the big bang theory). They have

had the truth right in front of them the whole time but refuse to acknowledge it.

> This only have I found:
> God created mankind
> upright, but they have gone
> in search of many schemes.
> (Ecclesiastes 7:29)

We have all this information at our fingertips. The proof is there if you truly want to know it. This is for keeps, this is your soul, and it's forever. Don't just roll the dice and hope that things will work out because they won't!

Who Is Jesus?

You may be asking, "Who is this Jesus anyway? That name that makes me uptight whenever I hear it. The name I use as a curse word." This is some guy who supposedly lived over 2,000 years ago. Someone who had some stories written about him in the Bible. A man who was said to have done a few miracles. A guy who upset the religious leaders of his day so much, they crucified him on a cross. They buried him in a tomb, and three days later, his body vanished. After this, some people said he had come back to life. They said they had seen him and talked with him. Wow, what a story. How is it that a story like this could ever even make it to our present time? You think a story like this would have fizzled out over the last 2,000 years, unless something supernatural was facilitating it. Why is there so much controversy over this one name? Controversy about who and what he actually is? Why is it the name of Jesus can bring about so many diverse reactions? Infuriating some at the mention of his name and bringing others so much peace.

There are several religious sects active in our present society that believe Jesus was a prophet of God, which in fact he was. That he came to point the people of the world back to God, which in fact he did. They give him credit for the miracles he performed while he was here: giving sight to the blind, restoring hearing to the deaf, healing the lame and crippled, casting demons from people, cleansing people from leprosy and many other diseases. Actually, even raising people from the dead. Some even giving him credit for creating life from a lump of clay. They give him credit for these things because there were so many witnesses to these impossible and miraculous feats. None of these things were ever done in secret. Even in the most private of moments, Jesus always brought with Him two to three witnesses. In his day, the law required at least two or three witnesses to establish the truth, in any matter. Many of the miracles Jesus performed were actually witnessed by hundreds and even thousands of people. They were also written down in scrolls and recorded as fact. There is no doubt there was absolutely something remarkable about this man. With all the witnesses and all the documentation recording all that Jesus said and did while he was here, it is easy to believe that he did actually exist and did some really awesome and impossible things.

Although many of these religious sects agree that Jesus was a prophet of God and had these awesome powers and authority, they don't agree on absolutely the most important aspect of Jesus's life and ministry. They don't agree that Jesus was the Son of God. Christianity is based on the fact that Jesus is the Son of God, the second person of the trinity: God the Father, God the Son (Jesus), and the Holy Spirit. One God represented in three distinct persons. If in fact Jesus is not God, all Christianity is absolutely worthless. If he wasn't God in the flesh, his sacrifice on the cross means nothing. That would mean there was no sacrifice that paid the sin debt for all humanity. This, according to the Bible, is the only sacrifice that could be made for the forgiveness of our sin. Without God himself making this sacrifice for us, all mankind is eternally condemned and without hope.

So what does the Bible and even the Quran actually have to say about this very critical issue? The Bible, the Quran, and other writings testify that Jesus was prophesied to come into the world. No other prophet or person, in all history, was prophesied to come into the world the way He did, by virgin birth. No other prophet was prophesied to do the things and perform the miracles he was prophesied to do. Starting with Abraham, Moses, David, and every other prophet mentioned in the Pentateuch, what we consider now as the Old Testament, all prophesied about Jesus. There are over five hundred prophecies in the Old Testament about the coming of Jesus. Many of these prophecies not only refer to Jesus as a prophet, they also refer to him many times as being the Son of God! According to the Bible, the Old Testament and the New, Jesus was the messiah who was prophesied to come into the world. The Messiah who would bring a new covenant to Israel, Judah, and the world.

Moses declares in the book of Deuteronomy 18:15, "The Lord your God will raise up for you a prophet like me from among you, from your brothers—it is to him you shall listen."

Hosea prophesying about the coming messiah, Jesus! "When Israel was a child, I loved him, and out of Egypt I called my son" (Hosea 11:1).

Jesus's parents, warned by an angel of God, fled to Egypt when he was a baby because King Herod was searching for him to kill him, which fulfills Hosea's prophecy.

> While the Pharisees were gathered round, Jesus put to them this question, "What is your opinion about the Christ? Whose Son, is he?" They told him, "David's." He said to them, "Then how is it that David, moved by the Spirit, calls him Lord, where he says: The Lord declared

to my Lord, take your seat
at my right hand, till I have
made your enemies your
footstool. If David calls him
Lord, how then can he be his
son?" (Matthew 22:41–45)

The prophet Isaiah, prophesying about
the coming messiah, refers to him as being
Mighty God.

For to us a child is born, to
us a son is given; and the
government shall be upon
his shoulder, and his name
shall be called Wonderful
Counselor, Mighty God,
Everlasting Father, Prince
of Peace. Of the increase of
his government and of peace
there will be no end. (Isaiah
9:5–7)

Now moving into the New Testament of
the Bible, which is basically a record of Jesus's
life and ministry, all written down by Jesus's

own disciples and several other eye witnesses, inspired by the Holy Spirit to record it in their own words. When the angel Gabriel appeared to Mary, sent by God to tell her she would be impregnated by the Spirit of God, which in fact was also prophesied hundreds of years earlier, he told her that Jesus would be called the Son of God!

> In the sixth month of Elizabeth's pregnancy, God sent the angel Gabriel to Nazareth, a town in Galilee, to a virgin pledged to be married to a man named Joseph, a descendant of David. The virgin's name was Mary. The angel went to her and said, "Greetings, you who are highly favored! The Lord is with you." Mary was greatly troubled at his words and wondered what kind of greeting this might be. But the angel said to her, "Do not be afraid, Mary;

you have found favor with God. You will conceive and give birth to a son, and you are to call him Jesus. He will be great and will be called the Son of the Most High. The Lord God will give him the throne of his father David, and he will reign over Jacob's descendants forever; his kingdom will never end." "How will this be," Mary asked the angel, "since I am a virgin?" The angel answered, "The Holy Spirit will come on you, and the power of the Most High will overshadow you. So, the holy one to be born will be called the Son of God. (Luke 1: 26–35)

The Quran calls Jesus the Word of God and the Spirit of God. The Bible also says the same thing with a little more detail.

In the beginning was the Word, and the Word was with God, and the Word was God. (John 1:1)

The Word became flesh and made his dwelling among us. We have seen his glory, the glory of the one and only Son, who came from the Father, full of grace and truth (Jesus). (John 1:14)

So if the scripture is true, which it absolutely is, and the Quran is true, the previous scripture and the Quran agree, stating that Jesus is the Word of God. It also states the Word was with God and the Word was God, which in fact makes Jesus God, who came in the flesh. I don't see how, after reading these passages in the scripture or even the Quran, anyone could come to any other conclusion. Even Jesus, on several occasions, talking about himself to his disciples and others, claims to be God.

Jesus answered, "I am the way and the truth and the life. No one comes to the Father except through me. If you really know me, you will know my Father as well. From now on, you do know him and have seen him." Philip said, "Lord, show us the Father and that will be enough for us." Jesus answered: "Don't you know me, Philip, even after I have been among you such a long time? (Anyone who has seen me has seen the Father). How can you say, 'Show us the Father'? Don't you believe that I am in the Father, and that the Father is in me? The words I say to you I do not speak on my own authority. Rather, it is the Father, living in me, who is doing his work. Believe me when I say that I am in the Father and the Father is in me; or at least believe on the evidence of the miracles themselves. Very truly I tell you, whoever believes in me will do the works I have been doing, and they will do even greater things than these, because I am going to the Father. And I will do whatever you ask in my name, so that the Father may be glorified in the Son. You may ask me for anything in my name, and I will do it. (John 14:6–14)

On another occasion, when Jesus was talking to a Samaritan woman at the well, Jesus had asked her to give him a drink. She was surprised he was even talking to her because in his day, a Jewish man was not allowed to associate with a Samaritan woman. During the conversation, Jesus himself claims to be the Messiah, the Christ who was to come. In the book of John, Jesus, speaking to the woman, says, "'God is spirit, and his worshipers must worship in the Spirit and in truth.' The woman said, 'I know the Messiah (called Christ) is coming. When he comes, he will explain everything to us.' Then Jesus declared, 'I, the one speaking to you, am he'" (John 4:24–26).

Why were the Jewish leaders so opposed to what Jesus said and did? Because he (Jesus) was claiming to be the Son of God. He was also introducing a brand-new covenant to the people, that through him alone is the only way to God. In him alone is our only hope for eternal salvation. Jesus was continually confronted by the Jewish leaders because they had no room for what Jesus was preaching and teaching. He did and said a lot of things that were not politically correct.

> So, because Jesus was doing these things on the Sabbath, the Jewish leaders began to persecute him. In his defense Jesus said to them, "My Father is always at his work to this very day, and I too am working." For this rea-

son they tried all the more to kill him; not only was he breaking the Sabbath, but he [Jesus] was even calling God his own Father, making himself equal with God.

Jesus gave them this answer: "Very truly I tell you, the Son can do nothing by himself; he can do only what he sees his Father doing, because whatever the Father does the Son also does. For the Father loves the Son and shows him all he does. Yes, and he will show him even greater works than these, so that you will all be amazed. For just as the Father raises the dead and gives them life, even so the Son gives life to whom he is pleased to give it. Moreover, the Father judges no one, but has entrusted all judgment to the Son, that all may honor the Son just as they honor the Father. Whoever does not honor the Son does not honor the Father, who sent him.

"Very truly I tell you, whoever hears my word and believes him who sent me has eternal life and will not be judged but has crossed over from death to life. Very truly I tell you, a time is coming and has now come when the dead will hear the voice of the Son of God and those who hear will live. For as the Father has life in himself, so he has granted the Son also to have life in himself. And he has given him authority to judge because he is the Son of Man.

"Do not be amazed at this, for a time is coming when

all who are in their graves will hear his voice and come out—those who have done what is good will rise to live, and those who have done what is evil will rise to be condemned. By myself I can do nothing; I judge only as I hear, and my judgment is just, for I seek not to please myself but him who sent me. (John 5:16–30)

Jesus, again defending himself to the Jewish leaders, says in John 5:36–47:

I have testimony weightier than that of John. For the works that the Father has given me to finish—the very works that I am doing—testify that the Father has sent me. And the Father who sent me has himself testified concerning me. You have never heard his voice nor seen his form, nor does his word dwell in you, for you do not believe the one he sent. You study the Scriptures diligently because you think that in them you have eternal life. These are the very Scriptures that testify about me, yet you refuse to come to me to have life. I do not accept glory from human beings, but I know you. I know that you do not have the love of God in your hearts. I have come in my Father's name, and you do not accept me; but if someone else comes in his own name, you will accept him. How can you believe since you accept glory from one another but do not seek the glory that comes from the only God?

> But do not think I will accuse you before the Father. Your accuser is Moses, on whom your hopes are set. If you believed Moses, you would believe me, for he wrote about me. But since you do not believe what he wrote, how are you going to believe what I say?

There were also three separate occasions recorded when God himself spoke and a voice came from heaven, proclaiming Jesus to be his Son. Again, there were a minimum of three witnesses on every occasion. On the first occasion, Jesus went to John to be baptized. God spoke from heaven calling Jesus his Son. Many witnesses were present.

> Then Jesus came from Galilee to the Jordan to be baptized by John. But John tried to deter him, saying, "I need to be baptized by you, and do you come to

me?" Jesus replied, "Let it be so now; it is proper for us to do this to fulfill all righteousness." Then John consented. As soon as Jesus was baptized, he went up out of the water. At that moment heaven was opened, and he saw the Spirit of God descending like a dove and alighting on him. And a voice from heaven said, "This is my Son, whom I love; with him I am well pleased." (Matthew 3:13–17)

On the second occasion, in more of a private moment, Jesus took three of his disciples who witnessed not only God speaking but Jesus being transfigured in front of them. Again, nothing Jesus did or said was done in secret. I believe he wanted everything to be established by at least two or three witnesses so there would be no question as to their validity.

After six days Jesus took Peter, James and John with him and led them up a high mountain, where they were all alone. There he was transfigured before them. His clothes became dazzling white, white like a flash of lightning. And there appeared before them Elijah and Moses, who were talking with Jesus. Peter said to Jesus, "Rabbi, it is good for us to be here. Let us put up three shelters—one for you, one for Moses and one for Elijah." He did not know what to say, they were so frightened. Then a cloud appeared and covered them, and a voice came from the cloud: "This is my Son, whom I love. Listen to him!" (Mark 9:2–7)

The third time, the voice came from heaven. Jesus knowing his crucifixion was just around the corner. God's voice was heard by a large crowd.

> Jesus replied, "The hour has come for the Son of Man to be glorified. Very truly I tell you, unless a kernel of wheat falls to the ground and dies, it remains only a single seed. But if it dies, it produces many seeds. Anyone who loves their life will lose it, while anyone who hates their life in this world will keep it for eternal life. Whoever serves me must follow me; and where I am, my servant also will be. My Father will honor the one who serves me. Now my soul is troubled, and what shall I say? 'Father, save me from this hour'? No, it was for this very reason I came

to this hour. Father, glorify your name!" Then a voice came from heaven, "I have glorified it, and will glorify it again." The crowd that was there and heard it said it had thundered; others said an angel had spoken to him. Jesus said, "This voice was for your benefit, not mine." (John 12:23–30)

These passages are just a few that have been recorded by eye witnesses of what Jesus said and did while he was here on the earth in human form. If you believe that Jesus came, if you believe in what Jesus said and did, if you believe Moses, if you believe the Pentateuch, if you believe what Moses wrote, if you believe Jesus was sent by God, there is no question he himself claimed to be the Son of God. He is so much more than just a prophet. His disciples, the men he lived with and trained, testify to the words he spoke and the miracles he did. They also witnessed the fact that he (Jesus) was actually crucified.

Jesus himself prophesied that he would be crucified. This is vitally important because there are some who claim it was not actually Jesus who was crucified. They claim (without any legitimate proof, I might add) that it was someone else crucified and Jesus was taken to heaven by God without dying. Honestly, that doesn't even make any sense. Why would the religious leaders crucify someone else? Jesus was the one who continually agitated them and threw them into chaos. It was Jesus that the High Priest and the council condemned because they said Jesus had blasphemed by calling himself the Son of God.

Jesus himself prophesied he would be crucified and that he would be raised to life after three days. This had also been prophesied hundreds of years earlier, that the Messiah would suffer and be crucified.

> Now Jesus was going up to Jerusalem. On the way, he took the Twelve aside and said to them, "We are going up to Jerusalem, and the Son of Man will be delivered

over to the chief priests and the teachers of the law. They will condemn him to death and will hand him over to the Gentiles to be mocked and flogged and crucified. On the third day he will be raised to life!" (Matthew 20:17–19)

There were also witnesses to the fact that he rose from the grave and appeared to them on several occasions. He presented himself first to Mary and then to the apostles. After that, he appeared to more than five hundred people at the same time.

After that, he appeared to more than five hundred of the brothers and sisters at the same time, most of whom are still living, though some have fallen asleep [died]. Then he appeared to James, then to all the apostles, and last of all he appeared to

me also, as to one abnor-
mally born. (1 Corinthians
15:6–8)

In my former book,
Theophilus, I wrote about
all that Jesus began to do
and to teach until the day he
was taken up to heaven, after
giving instructions through
the Holy Spirit to the apostles he had chosen. After his
suffering, he presented himself to them and gave many
convincing proofs that he
was alive. He appeared to
them over a period of forty
days and spoke about the
kingdom of God. On one
occasion, while he was eating with them, he gave them
this command: "Do not
leave Jerusalem, but wait for
the gift my Father promised,
which you have heard me
speak about. For John bap-

tized with water, but in a few day's you, will be baptized with the Holy Spirit."

Then they gathered around him and asked him, "Lord, are you at this time going to restore the kingdom to Israel?"

He said to them: "It is not for you to know the times or dates the Father has set by his own authority. But you will receive power when the Holy Spirit comes on you; and you will be my witnesses in Jerusalem, and in all Judea and Samaria, and to the ends of the earth."

After he said this, he was taken up before their very eyes, and a cloud hid him from their sight.

YOU ARE ALREADY DEAD

> They were looking intently up into the sky as he was going, when suddenly two men dressed in white [angels] stood beside them. "Men of Galilee," they said, "why do you stand here looking into the sky? This same Jesus, who has been taken from you into heaven, will come back in the same way you have seen him go into heaven." (Acts 1:1–11)

No other prophet was prophesied to come after Jesus except those Jesus himself said, would be false prophets and anti-Christs. Jesus said when he was hanging on the cross, "It is finished." He did say though many false prophets would come and that many anti-christs would come to deceive the world.

> I do not write to you because you do not know the truth, but because you do know it and because no lie comes

from the truth. Who is the liar? It is whoever denies that Jesus is the Christ. Such a person is the antichrist—denying the Father and the Son. No one who denies the Son has the Father; whoever acknowledges the Son has the Father also. (1 John 2:21–23)

This is Jesus! A man who was prophesied to come into the world as the Son of God, God in the flesh, hundreds of years in advance. The only man in all history prophesied to be and documented to have been born of a virgin. A man who walked this earth, healing the sick and diseased, giving sight to the blind, raising people from the dead. All prophesied, again, hundreds of years in advance that the Christ (Jesus) would do. Preaching to people to turn from their sinful ways and turn back to God. Prophesied that he would be crucified on a cross to pay the sin debt of all humanity. Prophesied to be placed in a borrowed tomb and after three days to be raised to life. Then taken to heaven in front of them all. He now sits on his throne at the right hand of God, interceding for all his people.

> Who then is the one who condemns? No one. Christ Jesus who died—more than that, who was raised to life—is at the right hand of God and is also interceding for us. (Romans 8:34)

Now we wait for his triumphal return, when he will return to the world just as prophesied. He will come not as the faithful servant, as he came before. This time, when he comes back, he will come back in great power and glory. The Bible says, when this happens, the whole world will see him. When he does return, the Bible also says, he is coming to take his faithful followers to their eternal, heavenly home.

> Immediately after the distress of those days the sun will be darkened, and the

moon will not give its light; the stars will fall from the sky, and the heavenly bodies will be shaken. Then will appear the sign of the Son of Man in heaven. And then all the peoples of the earth will mourn when they see the Son of Man coming on the clouds of heaven, with power and great glory. And he will send his angels with a loud trumpet call, and they will gather his elect (Christians) from the four winds, from one end of the heavens to the other. (Matthew 24:29–31)

Enter through the narrow gate. For wide is the gate and broad is the road that leads to destruction, and many enter through it. But small is the gate and narrow the road that leads to life, and

only a few find it. (Matthew
7:13–14)

His awesome return could happen at any
moment. When he comes back for his faithful followers. Only God the Father knows the
day and the hour it will happen. Don't be one
of the many, who are not ready for his return.
Once he comes, it's too late. Don't be one of
the many who will be left behind.

The Sacrifice

We have already discussed some of the story of Adam and Eve. I'm sure, or at least I would hope, most people in America have heard the story. How God created them, put them in the garden of Eden. They ate the forbidden fruit and were cursed. Most people, I don't believe, understand the true ramifications of what really happened to them and all mankind, when they ate that forbidden fruit. In the beginning, after Adam and Eve had committed what is referred to as the original sin. Animal sacrifice was instituted by God for the remission of sin. A perfect, non-blemished lamb or animal was selected from the flock, was killed and sacrificed on the altar as a burnt offering to God. The animal's blood was then sprinkled on the person who had offered the sacrifice as an atonement for their sin.

> Only by blood can sin be atoned for, for without blood there can be no forgiveness of sins. (Hebrews 9:22)

This type of sacrificial offering was made year after year for thousands of years. The offering was given to atone for that individual's sins. This blood sacrifice was instituted to cleanse the conscience of men for their sin. But no matter how many times it was offered, it could not change the sinful, diseased state of man's spirit.

> The law is only a shadow of the good things that are coming—not the realities themselves. For this reason, it can never, by the same sacrifices repeated endlessly year after year, make per-

fect those who draw near to
worship. (Hebrews 10:1)

Remember the passage that said we must
be holy even as our father in heaven is holy.
Without holiness or perfection, none of us
will ever enter heaven.

> Make every effort to live in
> peace with everyone and to
> be holy; without holiness
> no one will see the Lord.
> (Hebrews 12:14)

So what this means is there must be a
sacrifice offered for men that somehow not
only cleanses us from our sin but also changes
our sinful nature. A sacrifice that makes us
perfect or holy in God's sight. The problem
with this is there is absolutely no offering or
sacrifice man could ever make that changes
our sinful nature and makes us perfect before
a holy God.

> The ransom for a life is costly, no payment is ever enough. (Psalm 49:8)

Without a major intervention, there is absolutely no hope for us. We are all going to end up in a very, very undesirable place. That's where God stepped in. He knew from the beginning that man would fall away, sin against him, and be eternally condemned. You may ask, well, if God is so powerful and all-knowing, then why didn't he stop it? God is a holy God and he loves us more than any of us can possibly know. He wants only good for us, but he is also a God who will not violate our free will. He is not going to force anyone to love him and serve him. Man chose to run away from him. Man chose to sin and violate God's laws. Because of these choices, man allowed death into the world, both spiritual and physical. So what do we do now? We are in really big trouble. As I said before, God loves us; he really, really loves us. After all, he is the one who created us.

> This is what the LORD says your Redeemer, who formed you in the womb: I am the LORD, the Maker of all things, who stretches out the heavens, who spreads out the earth by myself. (Isaiah 44:24)

The holy God who created it all, the one who breathed his own breath into us, the one who gave us life. He created us because he wanted to have a relationship with us. He wants to love us, and he wants us to love him. But he will not force us. We have to decide to love him on our own accord. Do you want to know how much he loves you? He loves you so much, he chose to make the sacrifice himself. The ultimate sacrifice that cleanses all mankind from our sin. The only sacrifice that could change our sinful nature and make us perfect in his sight. The sacrifice that saves all mankind from an eternity in hell. Eternally separated from the God who formed us. God knew that no sacrifice man could ever make could possibly save us. That's when he sent his own son, Jesus, to be sacrificed as our sacrificial lamb. To shed his own blood, to die in our place, to pay the eternal penalty for our sin.

> For God so loved the world that He gave his one and only son, that whosoever believes on Him should not perish but have eternal life. For God did not send his Son into the world to condemn the world, but to save the world through him. Whoever believes in him is not condemned, but whoever does not believe stands condemned already because they have not believed in the name of God's one and only Son. (John 3:16–18)

This is one of the scriptures that tells us we are already dead without his sacrifice. This ultimate sacrifice is the only sacrifice that could cleanse us, change our sinful nature, and make us perfect in God's sight. Jesus chose to offer himself as that perfect sacrifice. That perfect, unblemished, sacrificial lamb.

> Very rarely will anyone die for a righteous person, though for a good person someone might possibly dare to die. But God demonstrates his own love for us in this: While we were still sinners, Christ died for us. (Romans 5:7–8)

You're telling me you want me to put all my hope for eternity in some guy who lived over 2,000 years ago? Yes, yes, I am! What other hope for your eternity are you holding on to? What proof do you have that what you are believing in is the real thing? The proof of who Jesus is and what he did for us is there. The eyewitness accounts have been meticulously recorded and preserved. All that we would have documented proof that Jesus is the true Son of God. This Jesus who gave His own life to save ours.

It was prophesied that he would be crucified on a cross. Then after three days, he would be raised from the dead. This fact was also witnessed again by hundreds of others, who also recorded the fact that they had seen Jesus after he had risen. Those who talked with him and ate with him. Those who touched him, even touching the holes in his hands and his side. The holes left in his flesh, where he was nailed to the cross and from a spear that pierced him, leaving a hole in his side. All these things again, prophesied hundreds and even thousands of years before they happened. All fulfilled to the tiniest detail. The Bible then says, Jesus was taken back into heaven. He ascended into heaven in front of them all. Witnessed again by hundreds of onlookers. The Bible says he now sits enthroned in heaven, sitting at the right hand of God, making intercession for all his people. He will remain there until the time for his second coming and the redemption of all his people.

> God has exalted him [Jesus] to his own right hand as ruler and savior, that he

might grant repentance to Israel [and the world] and grant forgiveness of sins. (Acts 5:31)

In the past God spoke to our ancestors through the prophets at many times and in various ways, but in these last days he has spoken to us by his Son, whom he appointed heir of all things, and through whom also he made the universe. The Son [Jesus] is the radiance of God's glory and the exact representation of his being, sustaining all things by his powerful word. After he had provided purification for sins, he sat down at the right hand of the Majesty in heaven. (Hebrews 1:1–3)

In your relationships with one another, have the same

mindset as Christ Jesus: Who, being in very nature God, did not consider equality with God something to be used to his own advantage; rather, he made himself nothing by taking the very nature of a servant, being made in human likeness. And being found in appearance as a man, he humbled himself by becoming obedient to death—even death on a cross! Therefore God exalted him to the highest place and gave him the name that is above every name, that at the name of Jesus every knee shall bow, in heaven and on earth and under the earth, and every tongue acknowledge that Jesus Christ is Lord, to the glory of God the Father. (Philippians 2:5–11)

Jesus chose to leave his royal place in heaven, humbled himself and became a man in the flesh. He was crucified on a cross. He took all the sin of the world upon himself. He went to hell for us, paid the penalty for all our sin, and by doing so purchased us a place in heaven.

> Surely he took up our pain and bore our suffering, yet we considered him punished by God, stricken by him, and afflicted. But he was pierced for our transgressions, he was crushed for our iniquities; the punishment that brought us peace was on him, and by his wounds we are healed. We all, like sheep, have gone astray, each of us has turned to our own way; and the LORD has laid on him [Jesus] the iniquity of us all. (Isaiah 53:4–6)

> This is love: not that we loved God, but that he loved us and sent his Son as an atoning sacrifice for our sins. (1 John 4:10)

He, by his sacrifice, made the only way for us to be forgiven. To be cleansed from all our sin and become children of God. If we choose to accept his sacrifice and accept Jesus as our Lord and Savior. We are then adopted by God as his children. He then actually sees us as he does Jesus, perfect, unblemished, and holy, completely forgiven. By his sacrifice, Jesus made us joint heirs with him to the kingdom of God. There are, however, stipulations to this sacrifice for sins. We do have to actually believe it.

> Peter replied, "Repent and be baptized, every one of you, in the name of Jesus Christ for the forgiveness of your sins. And you will receive the gift of the Holy Spirit." (Acts 2:38)

What that word *repent* means is, we have to turn from our old way of life. Turn away from our old sinful ways. We have to accept Jesus, as our Savior and the Lord of our lives. Once we do this, his spirit literally comes and inhabits us. His spirit comes to live inside us, to seal us as his children. He also promises to lead and guide us until the day we go to be with him in heaven, forever.

> God has said, "I will never leave you; I will never abandon you." (Hebrews 13:5)

> John answered them all, "I baptize you with water. But one who is more powerful than I will come, the straps of whose sandals I am not worthy to untie. He [Jesus] will baptize you with the Holy Spirit and fire. (Luke 3:16)

Romans 10:9 says, "If you declare with your mouth, 'Jesus is Lord,' and believe in your heart that God raised him from the dead, you will be saved."

You may be thinking, "I'm too far gone, I have sinned way too much. I have sinned in ways that God could never forgive. I can't even forgive myself." The scripture says whoever believes in him will be saved. *Whoever* means everyone, including you! It doesn't matter how bad you were in the past. If you accept his gift, he has forgiven you! Jesus, even while hanging on the cross, with spikes in his hands and feet, bleeding and dying, forgave those who crucified him. If he could forgive them, there is no doubt, he can forgive you.

> When they came to the place called the Skull, they crucified him there, along with the criminals—one on his right, the other on his left. Jesus said, "Father, forgive them, for they do not know what they are doing." And they divided up his clothes by casting lots. (Luke 23:33–34)

We cannot just believe that a man named Jesus existed, did some miracles, was crucified and died. We also cannot earn it. We can't work hard enough or do enough good things to earn it. It is the gift of God.

> For it is by grace you have been saved, through faith— and this is not from your-selves, it is the gift of God— not by works, so that no one can boast. (Ephesians 2:8–9)

We must actually believe that Jesus is the Son of God. He was begotten of God. He left his place in heaven, came to the earth that he created, was born of a virgin (Mary). He became a man, the only perfect man, the only sinless man to ever live. He gave his life on a cross and bore all our sins upon himself. He went to hell in our place, paid the penalty for all our sin, past, present, and future. After three days, he rose from the dead. He then ascended to heaven and sat at the right hand of God, making intercession for all his peo-ple. God is not judging us as many people may think he is. True Christians, and I did say *true* Christians, those who have a correct understanding, are not judging other people, as some may think. It may sound that way to some if they don't have the information that you just learned.

We as true Christians are really just trying to state the condition of *all* mankind. That we are all sinners. That we are *all* already condemned. We are *all* already dead spiritually, as the title of the book says. We want people to know that God has made the only way for us to be saved from that horrible eternity in hell. As a Christian, our job is to try and let people know how they can avoid this. For instance, if you had a friend who was walking in front of a speeding train and they did not see it, you know if you don't say or do something, that person is going to be run over and killed. Would you just stand there and let them get run over? No! You would probably be yelling and screaming. You would be jumping up and down and waving your arms frantically. You would do anything you could to keep them from that horrible outcome even if people thought you were a little crazy, as they thought Noah to be. This is what God tells us as Christians to do. To be his voice, to be his hands, to be his feet. To shout out to a fallen world that they are lost, that they are heading for disaster. Even when people think we're a little crazy. God has done everything He could do to save us. He does not want us to be condemned. He loves us. How many of us would give up our only child, condemn him, and sentence them to death to save someone else? None of us would, but that's exactly what he did for us.

> And from Jesus Christ, who is the faithful witness, the firstborn from the dead, and the ruler of the kings of the earth. To him who loves us and has freed us from our sins by his blood. (Revelation 1:5)

How much more could he possibly do to show you how much he loves you? How much more could he do to save us? How much more could he give?

What Does It Mean to Be a Christian

What does it mean to be a Christian? Well, we talked in the chapter on the sacrifice. That according to the Bible, there is only one way, one sacrifice for sin that could pay the penalty for our sin. One sacrifice, that could actually change our sin nature and make us perfect in God's eyes: Jesus's sacrifice on the cross as our sacrificial lamb. Him dying in our place and paying the penalty for our sin. That he is the only way we could ever be saved from an eternity in hell. And if we accept Jesus's sacrifice and accept Jesus as our Lord and savior, then we would be saved.

They replied, "Believe in the Lord Jesus, and you will be

saved—you and your house-
hold." (Acts 16:31)

This belief in and our yielding to Jesus constitutes us being a Christian. This in church circles is commonly known as being born again. You have died to your old way of life. Your old sin nature has died, you have been reborn into Christ. This is the reason Christians are baptized. It is an outward gesture, symbolizing the faith we now have in Jesus.

> For you have been born again, not of perishable seed, but of imperishable, through the living and enduring word of God. (1 Peter 1:23)

Christianity definitely does not mean you will become instantly perfect, or ever perfect for that matter. The only man who ever walked this earth perfect and without sin was Jesus. You don't become some self-righteous, holier than thou, religious fanatic either. Someone who becomes better than everyone else, as many people may think. Becoming a Christian doesn't even mean you have to become religious. Trying to look and act religious is way too much work. It surely doesn't mean you will never sin again either. You do again, repent of your acts of sin, and turn away from your old, sinful way of life. What it means is you have accepted the free gift of God's grace and mercy, that we have truly accepted Jesus into our hearts and lives as the only atoning sacrifice for our sin. We have made him our savior and the Lord of our life. We trust that his sacrifice on the cross has cleansed us from all our sin, past, present, and future. We have been adopted as sons and daughters of God himself.

> The Spirit you received does not make you slaves, so that you live in fear again; rather, the Spirit you received brought about your adoption to sonship. And by him we cry, "Abba, Father" [which means daddy]. (Romans 8:15)

God knows we still live in a sinful, corrupted body, and we still have a sinful, worldly mind to overcome. In other words, God knows we are still going to mess up. He knows we are still going to sin and chooses to love us anyway. He then starts to change us on the inside. He starts to turn our hearts and minds from a sinful, worldly mind-set to a heart and mind searching out the things of God.

> Since, then, you have been raised with Christ, set your hearts on things above, where Christ is, seated at the right hand of God. (Colossians 3:1)

This process of changing us is called sanctification. Sanctification is a lifelong process. It starts the moment you accept Jesus as your Lord and Savior and will continue until the day you die. This is where God starts to renew our hearts and minds, through his Word (the Bible), prayer, church, and other Christian people he will place into your life.

Basically, God starts to reprogram us, getting rid of the worldly garbage we have accumulated all our lives and replacing it with godly stuff. This process is something that we also have to work on. It will take discipline and work on our part, studying the Bible, praying, going to church, etc. Even Jesus said he sanctified himself so that through him, we would be sanctified.

> For them I sanctify myself, that they too may be truly sanctified. (John 17:19)

> For you know what instructions we gave you by the authority of the Lord Jesus. It is God's will that you should be sanctified: that you should avoid sexual immorality; that each of you should learn to control your own body in a way that is holy and honorable. (1 Thessalonians 4:2–4)

> Do not conform to the pattern of this world but be transformed by the renewing of your mind. Then you will be able to test and approve what God's will is— his good, pleasing and perfect will. (Romans 12:2)

The goal is, as we go through this renewal process, we will start to put aside our sinful, worldly desires. We will succumb to sin less and less and become more like Jesus in our actions, attitudes, and our works. In my experience, the more Bible we read, the more of God we put into our lives. The more we seek him, the more of him we will want. If we're not faithful to seek him consistently, the less we put in, the less of him we want. The devil again is very shrewd. He will come and try to snatch away what was sown into our hearts.

> When anyone hears the message about the kingdom and does not understand it, the evil one comes and snatches

away what was sown in their heart. This is the seed sown along the path. (Matthew 13:19)

The more we inundate our spirit with the things of God, the quicker he will be able to free us from our worldly attitudes and actions. Some people, though, may have areas of their lives that can be much harder for them to overcome. These areas may take a much longer time to get freed from or sanctified. God can and does deliver people instantly from some of those strongholds and bad habits that have had a grip on them. Some of those lifelong habits, though, they may still struggle with as a thorn in their side for the rest of their life. The consequences of our previous sinful life can still adversely affect us, even as a Christian.

These things, I believe, are sometimes what an unsaved person may see in a Christian's life, especially in young Christians, and will attribute this to them being a hypocrite. There are also many, many people out there who claim to be Christians and are not. I heard a statistic a few years ago that stated approximately 80 percent of Americans claimed to be Christian. I believe most of these people are deceived and don't have a correct understanding of what it is to be a true Christian. The devil uses these people to confuse and deceive the world and cause division in the churches. The devil wants you to think you are saved; he wants you to think you are okay. This group of people is also, most likely, the ones that he uses to cause others to think Christians are hypocritical.

> Watch out for false prophets. They come to you in sheep's clothing, but inwardly they are ferocious wolves. By their fruit you will recognize them. Do people pick grapes from thorn bushes, or figs from thistles? Likewise, every good tree bears good fruit, but a bad tree bears bad fruit. (Matthew 7:15–17)

What this means is, if someone is claiming to be a Christian but is consistently not behaving in a manner befitting a man or woman of God, they probably aren't. True Christians may have moments of weakness and may falter at times in their struggle against sin, but generally, it's not a lasting characteristic of a person who is truly trying to serve God.

> Not everyone who says to me, "Lord, Lord," will enter the kingdom of heaven, but only the one who does the will of my Father who is in heaven. Many will say to me on that day, "Lord, Lord, did we not prophesy in your name and in your name drive out demons, and in your name perform many miracles?" Then I will tell them plainly, "I never knew you. Away from me, you evildoers!" (Matthew 7:21–23)

Just because a person claims to be a Christian, does not make them one. Just because you sit in church all your life or belong to a church denomination, whether you claim to be Catholic, Methodist, Baptist, Lutheran, or any other denomination, does not make you a Christian. Just because your father and mother are Christians, does not make you one. You can even be a priest or a preacher or have a prominent position in a church. Even that does not make you a Christian. If you don't believe that statement, reread the previous scripture.

Praying to mother Mary, praying to any god, prophet, the angels or anyone or anything other than our Lord and Savior changes absolutely nothing. It also does not get you into heaven. Confession to a priest and chanting "Hail Mary's" does not forgive you of your sin. Having last rights pronounced over you before you die does not save your soul. Confessing our sin to someone else is a good thing but does not absolve us from anything. No one other than our Lord and God is deity. No one or nothing else in heaven or earth can forgive you of your sin and change your sin nature. Only Jesus can do this.

For in Christ [Jesus] all the fullness of the Deity lives in bodily form. (Colossians 2:9)

Only in God does my soul find rest; For salvation comes from him alone. (Psalm 62:1)

You need to be very careful who you follow. Just as the priests, teachers, and leaders of the church in Jesus's day were deceived and leading people astray, the devil has also placed leaders in some churches today who are doing the same things.

See to it that no one takes you captive through hollow and deceptive philosophy, which depends on human tradition and the elemental spiritual forces of this world rather than on Christ. (Colossians 2:8)

> Woe to you experts in the law, because you have taken away the key to knowledge. You yourselves have not entered, and you have hindered those who were entering. (Luke 11:52)

True born-again Christians are a small minority in this country, a remnant. I believe there are true Christians out there sitting in all types of church denominations. Many of these churches calling themselves Christian, unfortunately though, are not teaching the whole gospel of Jesus Christ. This will limit the effectiveness of the church and those sitting under this type of leadership. It can also limit you in your own personal Christian walk. This type of subtle deception can also keep people from coming to know Christ Jesus, as their Lord and Savior. Don't just settle for what is being taught by your leaders. Search the Bible diligently to make sure that what you are being taught is truly biblical. For your own sake, make sure nothing is being left out and nothing is being allowed into your church that is unbiblical.

> Dear friends, do not believe every spirit, but test the spirits to see whether they are from God, because many false prophets have gone out into the world. (1 John 4:1)

> For the time will come when people will not put up with sound doctrine. Instead to suit their own desires, they will gather around them a great number of teachers to say what their itching ears want to hear. (2 Timothy 4:3)

I also believe there are many who have given their hearts to the Lord. Those who truly want to live for Jesus and serve him but still, again, struggle with sin in some areas of their lives. Some of those past sins can have become so ingrained in their minds and hearts, they have become strongholds and bondages. These areas of struggle can sometimes cause Christians a lot of self-condemnation. God understands all this. He understands some of these strongholds can be very hard to overcome, some may take years. Some of these areas of sin and bondage, they may take to their grave. Their hearts may be right with God. They truly want to live for and serve him but still struggle in some areas.

Even King David, arguably the most well-known of Israel's kings, a man responsible for writing many of the Bible's prophecies and psalms. Jesus's human lineage was even traced from David. If you read about King David's life in the Bible, you see a man who messed up repeatedly in his walk with God, in his personal life, and in his reign as Israel's king. He was human just like you and me, and he struggled in several areas of his life, just as we do. Even with all his many failures and areas of disobedience, God himself called David a man after God's own heart. I believe that's what God really wants from us. To seek him, serve him, love him, and trust him to the best of our ability, in increasing measure.

But seek first his kingdom
and his righteousness, and
all these things will be given
to you as well. (Matthew
6:33)

God knows we live in an evil, fallen world. We live in a corrupted body and have worldly, sinful minds. Even though he knows all of this, he chooses to love us and work in us through these things, even if it takes him our entire life. His ultimate goal is to shape us and mold us into the image of his son Jesus Christ. He did all this to save our souls from an eternity in hell. He did all this so we could regain the fellowship with him, the fellowship Adam and Eve severed in the garden. That personal, intimate relationship with him, he wants to have with us here and now. He also wants us to be able to walk through this life with his peace and joy, not in fear. Then when we do face our ultimate earthly destiny, death, we will have the assurance, we have an eternal place with him in heaven.

> And you also were included
> in Christ when you heard the
> message of truth, the gospel
> of your salvation. When you
> believed, you were marked in
> him with a seal, the promised
> Holy Spirit, who is a deposit
> guaranteeing our inheri-
> tance until the redemption
> of those who are God's pos-
> session—to the praise of his
> glory. (Ephesians 1:13–14)

So what is our purpose as a Christian? God's ultimate purpose for us as Christians is not necessarily to make our lives easy. For us to just live in prosperity and never have problems. On the contrary, in John 16:33, Jesus said, "In this world you will have tribulation [troubles, problems, struggles, trials, etc.] but take heart [do not be troubled or worried] for I have overcome the world."

If we do have problems or troubles, which we will, he is faithful, he is in it with us. He is right there with you in every circumstance. In my experience, we tend to learn and grow more in our trials and troubles than we do when everything is going our way.

> Consider it pure joy, my brothers and sisters, whenever you face trials of many kinds, because you know that the testing of your faith produces perseverance. Let perseverance finish its work so that you may be mature and complete, not lacking anything. (James 1:2–4)

> The LORD himself goes before you and will be with you; he will never leave you nor forsake you. Do not be afraid; do not be discouraged. (Deuteronomy 31:8)

He has also promised to use everything we face in this life, every good and bad thing, to mold us and shape us more and more into the image of Jesus.

In Romans 8:28, his Word says, "*All* things work for the good of those who love the Lord, and who are called to his purpose."

All those bad things that may happen to us, those health problems, our financial problems, those problems at work, all those seemingly bad experiences, even a death in the family—everything we may deal with from the moment we give our lives to him, he has promised he will somehow use them all for our good, for our betterment. We may not know why or understand why he allows some things into our lives until we get to heaven. Sometimes we will just need to trust in him and know that there is a purpose for it all. This promise is for his children, for those who have accepted Jesus as their Lord and Savior.

God is not interested in just giving us a life of ease. He is much more interested in molding us and shaping us into people he can use to do his work. To further expand the Kingdom of God. To save other lost souls from an eternity in hell, eternally separated from the one who created us. He does not cause the evil in our lives. Along with the devil, we do that really well all by ourselves.

He will, though, allow both bad and good into our lives as he sees fit. He will use it all to make us more like him. Through this process, hopefully, we will allow him to make us wiser, more loving, more understanding, and more productive in the things of God. He will do all this through the power of his Holy Spirit that now indwells us.

If we allow him, he can use us to make a real difference in other people's lives. He is again sanctifying us so that we can be ministers to our families first, then to everyone he brings into our sphere of influence. This that others may have the opportunity to accept Jesus and be saved as well. I truly believe this book is God-inspired. I would never have chosen to write a book. God placed the burden of writing it on my heart a long time ago. This is not something I would have done on my own because, believe me, I am not a writer. I felt this was something he placed into me that I had to do. It took him a long time to get me to the place of spiritual maturity where he could use me in this way. Not because he is slow, but because I am. My desire for this book is that you and multitudes of others would come to know Jesus as their Lord and Savior, through what you read in it. That God through the Holy Spirit will free you from the fear of death. That you also will find freedom in Christ.

We as Christians are to be Jesus to all those the Lord brings into our path. Anywhere he may place us. At our jobs, where we live, where we play, where we shop, etc. I believe he has placed us there to be a light and a witness of what he has done in our lives. If you are openly claiming to be a Christian, believe me when I tell you people are watching you. They are watching to see if there really is something different in you. They are watching to see if you are really living what you are preaching.

> In the same way, let your light shine before others, that they may see your good deeds and glorify your Father in heaven. (Matthew 5:16)

As an old pastor of mine used to say, bloom where God has planted you! I don't believe anything happens by chance. God orchestrates everything in our lives for our sanctification and for the furthering of the gospel of Jesus Christ. I believe when we are truly striving to be as faithful as we can be in whatever circumstance we may find ourselves, when we do bloom where God has planted us, he is then able and willing to advance us into bigger, better, and more important things.

In Luke 16:10, it says, "A man that is faithful in the little things can also be trusted with much."

The whole Christian walk comes down to love, his love. Loving our fellow man enough to let them know we are all lost without Christ. That's what this book is about. Letting those who God has placed into my sphere of influence know we are all walking in front of that speeding train, heading for eternal disaster. The whole gospel is summed up in this one scripture.

Love the Lord your God
with all your heart and with

> all your soul and with all
> your strength and with all
> your mind; and, Love your
> neighbor as yourself. (Luke
> 10:27)

> This is love: not that we
> loved God, but that he loved
> us and sent his Son as an
> atoning sacrifice for our sins.
> (1 John 4:10)

Jesus loved us first. Again, he loved you so much that he gave his life for you. He was crucified on a cross for you. He took your place in hell and paid the penalty for you. If you had been the only person on this earth, he still would have done it all, just for you. The whole Christian walk is all about love. Nothing else can make as much difference in our lives and in this world as true love. The world would not have the troubles we see all around us if we would allow God's love to flow in and through us. There would be no more suicide, no more rape, no more murders, no more theft, no more pornography, no more need for drugs, no more sexual sin and perversion, no more divorce, etc. Love covers a multitude of sin.

> Let no debt remain outstanding, except the continuing debt to love one another, for whoever loves has fulfilled the law. (Romans 13:8)

This is sometimes very hard to do in this corrupted world we live in. We will sometimes have more compassion for dogs and cats than we do for our fellow man. Why? Because people hurt other people. People in their fallen, sinful state can be extremely selfish, self-centered, self-absorbed; they tend to care more about themselves than anyone or anything else. So sometimes it can be very hard to love people. We as Christians, though, need to remember that our struggle is not with man, but with the devil.

> For our struggle is not against flesh and blood, but against the rulers, against the

> authorities, against the powers of this dark world and against the spiritual forces of evil in the heavenly realms. (Ephesians 6:12)

> Love does not envy, love does not boast, love does not gossip, love does not condemn for obvious faults, love does not judge one another. (1 Corinthians 13:4)

We really don't know what is going on in another person's heart anyway; only God knows that. To sum it up, love does no harm! So no matter what others may be saying or doing around us or how much we may disagree, we should show love. This is probably the best witness we have as Christians.

> They will know we are Christians by our love for one another. Love is the fulfillment of the law. (John 13:34–35)

So love each other as Christ loved the church. He loved us enough that he laid down his life for us. He did not condemn us for our faults or judge us for our sin. He loved, even as he was being crucified on a cross!

What Now?

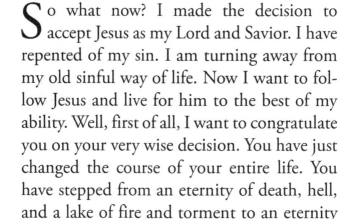

So what now? I made the decision to accept Jesus as my Lord and Savior. I have repented of my sin. I am turning away from my old sinful way of life. Now I want to follow Jesus and live for him to the best of my ability. Well, first of all, I want to congratulate you on your very wise decision. You have just changed the course of your entire life. You have stepped from an eternity of death, hell, and a lake of fire and torment to an eternity full of life, love, peace, and joy. You are now considered by God as one of his children. You are now eternally forgiven and are assured a place with all his children in heaven.

> They will be his people, and God himself will be with

them and be their God. He will wipe every tear from their eyes. There will be no more death or mourning or crying or pain, for the old order of things, has passed away. He who was seated on the throne said, "I am making everything new!" (Revelation 21:3–5)

Now take a deep breath, relax, and know that when you leave this world behind, even if it is today, you are going to spend eternity in a heavenly paradise with your Lord and Savior, Jesus Christ, the one who saved you. Let the peace of knowing God, or now being known by God, wash over you. You are forgiven! Forgiven for it all. Every sin, past, present, and future. You are now sealed by God as one of his own forever. You are sealed by his Holy Spirit, who now lives in you.

And do not grieve the Holy Spirit of God, with whom you were sealed for the day

of redemption. (Ephesians
4:30)

Now the Bible says to seek the face of God.

My heart says of you, "Seek
his face!" Your face, LORD,
I will seek. (Psalm 27:8)

When the Bible says, "My heart says to
seek his face," it is talking about the spirit
now inside you. It is telling you to search out
the things of God. To seek to truly know him.
To find out as much as you can about your
Lord and Savior, Jesus Christ. The more we
seek him, the more we will know him. The
more we know him, the more we will trust
him. The more we trust him, the more we
will yield to him. As we seek him diligently,
the more knowledge and understanding he
will be able to impart to us. As all this happens in us, the more useful and productive we
will become. This is all a lifelong process.

But seek first his kingdom
and his righteousness, and

all these things will be given
to you as well. (Matthew
6:33)

To do this, we need to start reading his
Word, the Bible. I would recommend starting
in the New Testament, maybe in the book of
John and go on from there. Don't worry about
understanding everything you read right now.
The Bible is the Word of God and has power.

For the word of God is alive
and active. Sharper than any
double-edged sword, it pen-
etrates even to dividing soul
and spirit, joints and mar-
row; it judges the thoughts
and attitudes of the heart.
(Hebrews 4:12)

As you read and pray, you are building up
and nourishing the spirit inside you. Just like
eating food nourishes the body and keeps us
strong and healthy, if we eat the right things,
reading the Bible nourishes our spirit and
keeps us strong. It's like putting on armor.

The Bible is an instruction book to help us live the Christian life as we should. It gives us examples of how others lived and triumphed over their world. Also, how some of them really messed up in life. The Bible is full of imperfect people whom God still loved and was still able to use to further the gospel. We are training ourselves to be more godly.

> Have nothing to do with godless myths and old wives' tales; rather, *train yourself to be godly*. For physical training is of some value, but godliness has value for all things, holding promise for both the present life and the life to come. This is a trustworthy saying that deserves full acceptance. (1 Timothy 4:7–9)
>
> Rejoice always, pray continually, give thanks in all circumstances; for this is God's

will for you in Christ Jesus.
(1 Thessalonians 5:16–18)

Praying and listening for God's voice is vital in seeking him and coming to know Him. How can you really know someone if you don't talk to them? If you don't spend quality time with them? Jesus is now and will always be there with you. He is real, he really hears you, and he really does talk to us. We just need to come to the place where we really listen.

> When he has brought out all his own, he goes on ahead of them, and his sheep follow him because they know his voice. (John 10:4)

We are the sheep this scripture is talking about. He will enable us to hear his voice. Praying is not some formal ritual you need to follow. Praying is just talking to him. Just like you would talk to a good friend. Because he is that and so very much more. Getting into a good church is also very important. I would recommend getting into a church that really worships the Lord in song. One that truly preaches and teaches the whole Bible. One that preaches and teaches Jesus. Get into a church where you feel comfortable. Getting around other Christians is also really important. People who will be able to mentor you, teach you, and admonish you in your walk with the Lord. All these things God uses to train us in our Christian walk.

The Christian walk is definitely not the easy way out. We unfortunately have an archenemy. We always have to be aware, there is a devil out there. He is always lurking and wants more than anything to trip you up. He will use any means possible to interfere with your newfound life in Christ. He will use your doubts, your fears, he will use other people, your family, even people in the church to get you off the right path.

> Watch out for false prophets. They come to you in sheep's clothing, but inwardly they are ferocious wolves. (Matthew 7:15)

Remember the passage that talks about your enemy, the devil, being like a roaring lion, going to and fro, throughout the whole earth, seeking someone to devour. As a Christian, he hates you! He wants nothing more than to destroy you. As a Christian though, you do not have to be afraid of him, or anything else that may come your way. As a child of God, he has given us power and authority in the name of Jesus.

> I have given you authority
> to trample on snakes and
> scorpions and to overcome
> all the power of the enemy;
> nothing will harm you.
> (Luke 10:19)

God has given you power and authority in the name of Jesus, but you still need to always be prepared for the devil's attacks. Even Jesus spent a great deal of time praying. He got away from everything often and prayed to the Father to keep his spirit charged. How do you get yourself prepared for those attacks and anything else that might come your way? The Bible calls it putting on the armor of God.

> Finally, be strong in the Lord and in his mighty power. Put on the full armor of God, so that you can take your stand against the devil's schemes. For our struggle is not against flesh and blood, but against the rulers, against the authorities, against the powers of this dark world and against the spiritual forces of evil in the heavenly realms. Therefore put on the full armor of God, so that when the day of evil comes, you may be able to stand your ground, and after you have done everything, to stand. Stand firm then, with the belt of truth buckled around your waist, with the breastplate of righteousness in place, and with your feet

fitted with the readiness that comes from the gospel of peace. In addition to all this, take up the shield of faith, with which you can extinguish all the flaming arrows of the evil one. Take the helmet of salvation and the sword of the Spirit, which is the word of God. And pray in the Spirit on all occasions with all kinds of prayers and requests. With this in mind. Be alert and always keep on praying for all the Lord's people. (Ephesians 6:10–18)

Wow, that sounds like a lot. How can I do all this? You stay in the Word. You read the Bible every day. Pray continually, talk to the Lord all day long, every time you think about it. Set aside a specific time to spend with him alone, just you and him. I like to do this in the morning, before I am inundated with the troubles and stresses of the day. I want to get my spirit charged up and ready for anything.

You want to stay in church to keep your spirit fed with the worship of the Lord in a corporate setting. We also need to stay in fellowship with other believers. Get involved in the church you choose. Get to know other believers; they will become your spiritual family. The devil will exploit any weakness that you have. So keep filling your spirit with the things of God. You might be thinking this sounds like a whole lot more than I signed up for. This is all a growing process, a lifelong process. God, through the Holy Spirit, will let you know what to change and when to change things in your life. The Holy Spirit inside you will lead and guide you, as you become more sensitive to his promptings and his voice.

> For the Spirit God gave us does not make us timid, but gives us power, love and self-discipline. (2 Timothy 1:7)

> The Lord himself goes before you and will be with you; he will never leave you

> nor forsake you. Do not be
> afraid; do not be discour-
> aged. (Deuteronomy 31:8)

You weren't born an adult. You were born a baby and grew up a little at a time. You started with your mother's milk and then grew into solid food. It's the same with the Christian walk. Just start small and work your way into deeper things as God leads. Start reading the Bible when you think you should. Start praying when you think you should. And find a true Bible-preaching church that you are comfortable in. Just take baby steps. God will work it all out; he already has an awesome plan for your life.

> "For I know the plans I have
> for you," declares the Lord,
> "plans to prosper you and
> not to harm you, plans to
> give you hope and a future."
> (Jeremiah 29:11)

You are now his child and are in his hands. He can see your past, your present, and your future. He is already there. He is the only one who will never let you down; no one else on this earth can promise you that. He said he will never leave you or forsake you; no one else can promise that either. So know from this point on you are never alone. You have his promise: he is going to be with you through it all. So just start seeking to know him and find out how much goodness he has in store for the rest of your life and your eternity.

About the Author

J erry Lee Johnson was born in Louisville, Kentucky, in 1962. He has been with his wife, Dianne, for over thirty-seven years. He is the father of four children who have given him nine awesome grandchildren. He has been living in the Seattle, Washington, area for the past ten years, working in retail sales. He has no formal training in writing or ministry but has been a born-again, Spirit-filled follower of Jesus Christ for a very long time. When asked to describe himself, he quoted the lyrics to a popular Christian song: "I am just a nobody, trying to tell everybody, about the somebody, who saved my soul." God placed the desire to write this book in him over twenty years ago, after the unexpected death of his oldest son, Quentin, taken at the young age of just twenty-five years. He states that very little of this book was written without being in fasting and prayer. This, to be as certain as possible, it was God's message he was hearing and writing down. He claims Jesus is the true author of this book and should receive all the credit, the praise, and the glory for the lives that will be saved and changed by reading it.

CPSIA information can be obtained
at www.ICGtesting.com
Printed in the USA
BVHW070812150221
600147BV00002B/121

9 781098 044305